THE DIEPPE RAID

THE ALLIES' ASSAULT UPON HITLER'S FORTRESS EUROPE, AUGUST 1942

THE DIEPPE RAID

THE ALLIES' ASSAULT UPON HITLER'S FORTRESS EUROPE, AUGUST 1942

John Grehan and Alexander Nicoll

Frontline Books

THE DIEPPE RAID
The Allies' Assault Upon Hitler's Fortress Europe, August 1942

First published in Great Britain in 2023 by Frontline Books,
an imprint of Pen & Sword Books Ltd,
Yorkshire – Philadelphia

Copyright © John Grehan and Alexander Nicoll
ISBN: 978-1-39906-720-1

The right of John Grehan and Alexander Nicoll to be identified as the Authors of this work has been asserted by them in accordance with the Copyright, Designs and Patents Act 1988. A CIP catalogue record for this book is available from the British Library All rights reserved.

No part of this book may be reproduced or transmitted in any form or by any means, electronic or mechanical including photocopying, recording or by any information storage and retrieval system, without permission from the Publisher in writing.

Typeset in 9.5/12.5 Avenir by Dave Cassan
Printed and bound by CPI UK

Printed on paper from a sustainable source by CPI Group (UK) Ltd, Croydon, CR0 4YY

Pen & Sword Books Ltd incorporates the imprints of Air World Books
After the Battle, Pen & Sword Archaeology, Atlas, Aviation, Battleground, Discovery, Family History, History, Maritime, Military, Naval, Politics, Social History, Transport, True Crime, Claymore Press, Frontline Books, Praetorian Press, Seaforth Publishing and White Owl.

For a complete list of Pen & Sword titles please contact:

PEN & SWORD BOOKS LTD
47 Church Street, Barnsley, South Yorkshire, S70 2AS, UK.
E-mail: enquiries@pen-and-sword.co.uk
Website: www.pen-and-sword.co.uk

Or

PEN AND SWORD BOOKS
1950 Lawrence Road, Havertown, PA 19083, USA
E-mail: Uspen-and-sword@casematepublishers.com
Website: www.penandswordbooks.com

CONTENTS

Acknowledgements — vi

Chapter 1 Europe First — 1
Chapter 2 Operation *Jubilee* — 13
Chapter 3 What Did the Germans Know? — 23
Chapter 4 Yellow Beach — 29
Chapter 5 Orange Beach — 35
Chapter 6 Blue Beach — 51
Chapter 7 Green Beach — 59
Chapter 8 Red and White Beaches — 65
Chapter 9 Tank Attack — 79
Chapter 10 The Aerial Battle at Dieppe — 101
Chapter 11 The Withdrawal — 131
Chapter 12 The Aftermath — 161

References and Notes — 193

ACKNOWLEDGEMENTS

The majority of the images used in this publication are from the Historic Military Press collection or are public domain, unless stated otherwise. In respect of the latter, the authors would like to extend their grateful thanks, in no particular order, to the following individuals and organisations for their assistance with the images used in this publication: Chris Goss (not only for his assistance with the images, but for information and quotes used in the text), Robert Mitchell, Dave Cassan, US Naval History and Heritage Command, the National Museum of the US Navy, the Canadian Department of Defence, Library and Archives Canada, the Toronto Public Library, US Library of Congress, the National Archives and Records Administration, the Danish National Museum, Polish National Archives, and the Bundesarchiv.

Chapter 1

EUROPE FIRST

The month of April 1942 marked in almost every theatre of war the nadir of Allied fortunes since the capitulation of France in 1940. In the Far East, the Japanese had so far carried all before them; Singapore, Hong Kong, Malaya and even Burma had fallen or were certain to fall to the Japanese and north-east India was in the balance. The pride of the British fleet, the battleship HMS *Prince of Wales*, along with the accompanying battlecruiser HMS *Repulse*, had been sunk. Some 4,000 miles further east, Japanese landings had taken place in East New Guinea; Australia felt herself gravely menaced. In the Middle East a German advance of some 300 miles in Cyrenaica had taken place in February; Admiral Sir Andrew Cunningham's Mediterranean Fleet, gravely weakened by recent casualties, was battling to protect the vital convoys to Malta, then undergoing savage air attack. It was against this backdrop that the idea of launching a raid of the French coastal resort of Dieppe was first considered.

Below: Britain had not been idle and had been conducting raids against German-held territory in Europe since 1940. One of these early raids was Operation *Claymore*, which was carried out against the Lofoten Islands on 4 March 1941. Taken during that operation, this image shows oil burning on the surface of the sea at Stamsund, which was attacked by No.3 Commando.

THE DIEPPE RAID

The origins of such a raid can be traced back to Monday, 22 December 1941. It was on that date, two weeks after the Japanese attack on the US Pacific Fleet at Pearl Harbor, that Prime Minister Winston Churchill arrived in Washington to meet President Roosevelt for the first time. The significance of the meeting between the two leaders, formalised as the Arcadia Conference, was the declaration of a policy of 'Europe First' for the direction of the war. Every effort would be made to defeat Germany while aiming to constrain the Japanese in the Pacific until the full weight of Allied arms could be turned eastwards. This suited the aims of both men.

Naturally, therefore, Roosevelt expected Britain and the United States to launch an attack upon Hitler's so-called 'Fortress Europe' at the earliest opportunity. Equally, now that America was on their side, so did the British public and press. But people perhaps did not understand just how precarious a position Britain was in during the early part of 1942. Her forces were in retreat across the globe and in no position whatsoever to mount a major operation across the Channel.

Yet without US support, particularly with regards to arms and equipment, Britain would be unable to continue its war against the Axis. So, what America wanted, America got.

On 9 March 1942, Roosevelt wrote to Churchill urging the consideration of an attack across the Channel. In this communication the American President declared that 'I am becoming more and more interested in the establishment of a new front this summer on the European continent'. Roosevelt went on to add that 'even though losses will doubtless be great, such losses will be compensated by at least equal German losses and by compelling the Germans to divert large forces of all kinds from the Russian front'.

In March 1942, Harry Hopkins, Roosevelt's closest political advisor, wrote to the President with these words: 'I doubt if any single thing is any more important as getting some sort of front this summer against Germany.' This was because of the upcoming mid-term elections by which time the Americans would expect to see some positive action being taken against the enemy. Roosevelt agreed that it was 'very important … to give this country a feeling that they are in the war' and that the Americans would soon have to start 'slugging' it out with the Germans.

In an attempt maintain the pressure on the British, Roosevelt despatched General George Marshall, the Chief of Staff of the US Army, and Harry Hopkins to the UK. Bringing with them details of two possible plans for Allied landings in Occupied France, the pair landed in Britain on 8 April.

The first of these schemes, Operation *Roundup*, was in many ways the original Allied plan for the invasion of continental Europe. It called for a force of forty-eight Allied divisions, supported by 5,800 aircraft, to undertake a series of landings on broad beachheads between the French ports of Boulogne and Le Havre. This, though, was almost laughably unrealistic in 1942 or 1943.

Senior British officers were able to persuade the Americans to scrap the idea. However, the continuing debate then centred on the second, considerably less ambitious, plan – Operation *Sledgehammer*. In this, the French ports of either Brest or Cherbourg would be assaulted during the early autumn of 1942 if Germany or the Soviet Union was on the brink of collapse.

Again, as most of the troops would have to be drawn from British or Commonwealth forces, because the US would only be able to provide two or three trained divisions in time, British leaders were able to put a stop to this proposal, with Churchill preferring an attack in North Africa and the

Left: Another of the early raids against German-held territory. Here, Lord Louis Mountbatten is pictured inspecting a number of Commandos before their departure to participate in Operation *Archery*, the Combined Operations raid on Vaagso and Måløy, which was undertaken on 27 December 1941. (National Museum of the US Navy)

THE DIEPPE RAID

Above: Commandos in action during Operation *Archery*, the Combined Operations raid on Vågsøy and Måløy in December 1941. (Danish National Museum)

Mediterranean, which he called Europe's 'soft underbelly'. He argued that in attacking North Africa the relatively inexperienced American forces would be able to gain experience in a less intense theatre before engaging the Germans head on in northern Europe.

Eventually, British reasoning won out and the Americans agreed to invade French North Africa before attempting a cross-Channel attack. This was Operation *Torch*. This, though, did not completely spike the Americans' push for some form of offensive in the north.

It was not just the US pressing for an attack on mainland Europe. The Soviet Union, the Prime Minister was told, was losing 10,000 men a day on the Eastern Front, whilst Britain, the Soviet Ambassador mocked, was dragging its heels 'until the last button has been sown on the tunic of the last soldier'.[1]

Such appeals had not gone unheeded in the West, as General Alan Brooke, the Chief of the Imperial General Staff, noted in his diary for 16 April: 'Public Opinion is shouting for the formation of a new Western Front to assist the Russians. But they have no conception of the difficulties and dangers entailed. The prospects of success are small and dependent on a mass of unknowns, whilst the chances of disaster are great and dependent on a mass of well-established facts. Should Germany be getting the best of an attack on Russia, the pressure or invasion of France will be at its strongest, and yet this is just the most dangerous set of circumstances for us.'[2] Brooke, Britain's

Above: One of the wounded raiders is assisted back to a landing craft during Operation *Archery*, 27 December 1941. (Danish National Museum)

most senior military figure, believed a premature landing in France 'could only result in the most appalling shambles'.[3]

Churchill had managed to bat away *Roundup* and *Sledgehammer*, but he knew he had to do something to appease the Americans, the Russians, the press and, it seemed, just about everybody else. When it was announced on 9 May that the Soviet Foreign Minister was coming to London, Churchill demanded something to present to Vyacheslav Molotov.

Four days later the head of Britain's Combined Operations, Lord Louis Mountbatten, presented an outline plan for a 'super-raid' upon the French port of Dieppe which would involve just one infantry division plus supporting troops. This was sufficiently limited in scale that Brooke could, albeit reluctantly, agree to and big enough for Churchill to be able to show that Britain was taking the Kremlin's appeals for help seriously.

Despite many questions still remaining unresolved at that stage, the plan was given the go-ahead. It was to be the largest cross-Channel of the raid of the war so far, and it would surely satisfy all those who demanded action.

The practicalities of mounting a raid on Dieppe were first investigated by the Target Committee of Combined Operations Headquarters in early April 1942, the task of devising an operational plan being handed to its Planning Staff under the general direction of Captain J. Hughes-Hallett RN. From the outset the idea of a frontal assault was rejected. Instead, it was proposed that a landing at brigade strength supported by tanks would be made on each flank – one at Quiberville, some six miles to the west of Dieppe, the other at Oriel-sur-Mer, about double the distance to the east. A third brigade would be held as a floating reserve to reinforce either flank or to land at Dieppe as the flanking brigades approached the town.

A few weeks earlier, on 30 March 1942, the Chiefs of Staff had given their approval for the military part of any plan for large Cross-Channel raids contingent upon its being agreed by a senior officer nominated by the Commander-in-Chief, Home Forces, who, at this point in the war, was Lieutenant General Bernard Montgomery. But Montgomery was far from impressed with the military plan that was being developed for Dieppe. In particular, he believed that the distance the flanking forces had to travel was too great for the RAF to be able to maintain aerial superiority, which was essential if the attack was to succeed. Instead, Montgomery said that Dieppe should be taken frontally in a dawn attack with two smaller landings either side to seize the cliffs which overlooked the town.

These competing assessments were appraised by the Chiefs of Staff. They broadly supported Montgomery's view, reasoning that the element of surprise would be lost once the flanking attacks landed, allowing the defenders in Dieppe to prepare for the eventual assault. The time taken by the flanking forces to reach Dieppe – especially with regards to the western approach where two streams would have to be crossed which might impede the tanks – would also enable the Germans to call up reinforcements, and delays in the capture of Dieppe would compromise the time/tidal constraints imposed upon the Navy. As a result, the decision was made to mount a frontal assault preceded by flank attacks at Puits (or Puys) and Pourville, while at the same time parachute and glider-borne troops would be used to capture the gun batteries at Berneval-le-Grand and Varengeville-sur-Mer.

The assault would be preceded by an aerial bombardment of 'maximum intensity' which would be carried out by 150 high-level bombers and four squadrons of low-level bombers. No less than sixty squadrons of fighters would provide aerial support for the flotilla of boats and for the troops during the raid itself. The raid would take place in daylight over two tides, a period of about twelve hours.

Eventually, it was a modified version of this plan which was given the green light by the Prime Minister and the Chiefs of Staff under the codename *Rutter*.

While the main reasons for mounting a large-scale assault upon Occupied France were primarily political, the troops were given sixteen specific objectives from which items had to be collected or which had to be captured and destroyed – see the side box. Whilst some of these objectives may, at first sight, appear trivial, as will be learned, two were in fact of considerable importance.

Despite the immediate reservations and concerns, there was no doubt that the Allies would invade Europe in 1943 or, more likely, 1944. There was also universal agreement that any operation of this kind would have to include the early capture of a port to allow supplies and reinforcements to be landed quickly. An attack upon the port of Dieppe would be an ideal practice for such an operation. The scale of the assault under *Rutter* would, it was also hoped, be large enough to appease all the concerned parties. It was a typically British compromise.

On 5 June a modification to the plan was introduced. It was decided to abandon the high-level bombing of Dieppe on air and military grounds: 'The Air Force Commander [Air Vice-Marshal T. Leigh-Mallory] was of the opinion that the bombing of the port itself during the night prior to the assault would not be the most profitable way to use bombers and might only result in putting the enemy on alert.' Similarly, Major-General J.H. Roberts, the Military Commander, took the view that the destruction of large numbers of houses and the setting of a considerable portion of the town on fire through bombing would probably prevent the tanks from operating in streets chocked with debris. Understandably, there was also a disinclination to bomb the homes and businesses of the innocent French civilians.

As an alternative to high-level bombing, Leigh-Mallory proposed that diversionary bombing attacks should be made on Boulogne and the airfields at Abbeville-Drucat and Crécy. This would have two advantages. The first of these was that the diversionary attacks would occupy the attention of the German radar network and secondly it would put out of action two of the closest Luftwaffe airfields.

It was also agreed that fighters should attack the beach defences and the high ground on either side of Dieppe, while the German Divisional Headquarters at Arques-la-Bataille, a few miles inland from Dieppe, should be bombed. The bombardment of Dieppe was now to be limited to the 4-inch guns of six destroyers and the 250lbs bombs of Hurricane fighter-bombers. A force of Motor Gun Boats was to operate off Boulogne in the early stages of the raid to give the impression that the assault would take place there instead of at Dieppe.

A period of intensive training followed, with the idea of carrying out the operation on the first favourable date after 24 June. The period when astronomical and tidal conditions were favourable was limited to some five or six days twice a month; and it had been accepted that settled fair weather for a period of at least forty-eight hours was necessary for the attack. Unfortunately, the weather proved uniformly unfavourable for the airborne troops though not consistently so for the beach landings, and on 5 July the operation was further postponed and the plan again altered. Parachute troops would no longer be involved, their place being taken by Commandos.

Owing to the changed states of the tides, troops would now have to be re-embarked three hours later than originally arranged. This necessitated three hours longer air cover and, in the opinion of the Military Commander, might give the enemy the opportunity to organize infantry and artillery opposition on a scale which might prejudice the re-embarkation. The Force Commanders therefore informed the Chief of Combined Operations that in their view the operation had a diminishing chance of success as each day passed and should not be carried out in its original form on the date proposed of 7 July. They were accordingly instructed to consider a modified plan whereby the operation would take place on one tide only.

TARGETS FOR THE ATTACKERS

1. Invasion craft consisting of converted barges and tank landing craft.
2. German Headquarters located in various hotels.
3. Gambetta barracks, and also barracks and coast guard station on the cliff at Puits.
4. The Casino, used as an ammunition dump.
5. Railways, marshalling yards, and tunnels.
6. Gas works and power station.
7. Pharmaceutical factory, the destruction of this was desirable in view of the shortage of these products in Germany.
8. Petrol tanks or dumps.
9. Bridges and locks.
10. Food stores at Bassin de Paris, used for German Army.
11. The Luftwaffe airfield at St. Aubin.
12. Dieppe's Town Hall.
13. The Radar station at Caude-Cote.
14. Post office in which was located the main telephone exchange.
15. E- and R-boats and Siebel ferries.
16. Area of town occupied by Germans.

THE DIEPPE RAID

Above: The Würzburg radar station at Bruneval on the French coast. It was reconnaissance photographs of this site, taken in January 1941, that led to plans for Operation *Biting* being drawn up. This resulted in another raid by British forces which was carried out on the night of 27/28 February 1942.

The landing was now to be made as near low water as possible and to be completed or nearly completed by the next high water. Though on the one hand this 'one tide' plan had the advantage of increasing the intensity of air support by shortening the time during which cover would have to be given, on the other hand it tended to complicate the task of removing the German barges in Dieppe harbour, which was one of the objects of the operation. The great raid was becoming smaller with the passing of every month.

If this was bad news for the assaulting forces, then worse was to come. The public debate concerning a second front had not gone unnoticed across the Channel. In the months leading up to

Operation *Rutter* the Germans had made significant improvements to their coastal defences and large numbers of reinforcements had been drafted in, some even being transferred from the Russian Front, to protect the French ports. On 20 July, the Joint Intelligence Sub-committee had informed the Chiefs of Staff that 'all ports are especially strongly defended. Defence of the coast will pivot on ports which will probably be converted into quasi-fortresses with all-round defence.'

Such, then, was the situation as the troops moved down to their embarkation points for the great raid. The invasion flotilla assembled in the Solent at the beginning of July and, on the 2nd of the month, the men involved were loaded on board. Operation *Rutter* would commence that night.

Then things started to go wrong. Adverse weather delayed the sailing of the flotilla. Day after day the troops waited on the weather reports until, on the morning of 7 July, the Luftwaffe made an appearance. A flight of four Focke-Wulf Fw 190s, each armed with machine-guns, 20mm cannon and a single high-explosive 500kg bomb, attacked the exposed vessels.

Two Landing Ships, Infantry (LSI) – HMS *Princess Astrid* and HMS *Princess Josephine Charlotte* – then lying in Yarmouth Roads, Isle of Wight, with troops embarked ready for the operation, were hit, the latter being severely damaged.

Hurried attempts were made to find alternative transports but by then it was too late. The tides had become unfavourable. There was also every possibility that the German pilots had reported they had seen a considerable build-up of shipping which, in light of concerns that the British might be about to launch a large-scale raid upon the French coast, would have further alerted the Germans to the possibility of an attack. The operation had become impractical and had almost certainly been compromised. The commanding officers had no choice, *Rutter* had to be cancelled.

But rather than the end of the story, this was just the beginning.

The cancellation of *Rutter* did not help Churchill, nor the ambitious Mountbatten, at all. Since taking over Combined Operations in October 1942, Mountbatten had overseen the raid on the dry dock at St Nazaire, which, while a success, was ultimately fruitless. The reason for the destruction of the dry dock was to force German warships to run the gauntlet of the Home Fleet in the Channel. Yet in the infamous 'Channel Dash' in February 1942 two German battleships and a heavy cruiser had steamed through the Channel to their home ports virtually unscathed.

Other raids proposed by Mountbatten in 1942 were cancelled by the Chiefs of Staff as being unviable. These included an attack upon Alderney, one on Bayonne, on Hardelot in the Pas-de-Calais (Operation *Abercrombie*), another on the Adour Estuary in south-western France (Operation *Myrmidon*), and an extremely ambitious plan to capture and hold the Cotentin Peninsula.

With the months passing by, Mountbatten had precious little to show his mentor Churchill. Mountbatten was supposed to 'turn the south coast of England from a bastion of defence into a springboard of attack … your whole attention is to be concentrated on the offensive'.[4]

But with the months slipping away and as there were no other cross-Channel raids on the table for 1942, Mountbatten did not want to lose the one operation which had received backing from the Chiefs of Staff. With this in mind Mountbatten was able to gain Brooke's acceptance that, as so much thought and planning had gone into *Rutter*, if there was to be any further consideration given to an attack upon the French coast that year, re-mounting it would be the easiest, quickest and most cost-effective option.

Overleaf: German prisoners captured during the attack on Bruneval, Operation *Biting*, being searched by some of the raiders.

THE DIEPPE RAID

Whatever would be decided, there would be limited involvement from either Brooke or Churchill as they were shortly afterwards on their way to Cairo and from there the two men and their advisory teams were to fly to Moscow. All that followed, therefore, happened while the senior political and military leaders were out of the UK. Mountbatten saw this as his chance and, on 12 July, he asked the Chiefs of Staff to consider mounting an operation to replace *Rutter*.

The senior military commander for *Rutter* had been General Montgomery, but he had been sent to Cairo to take charge of the Eighth Army. Similarly, the Naval Force Commander for *Rutter*, Rear Admiral Harold Baille-Grohman had also been moved on to another posting. *Rutter*'s Air Force commander, Air Vice Marshal Trafford Leigh-Mallory was only interested in bringing the Luftwaffe to battle at a time and place of his choosing, and if that meant Dieppe, that that was fine with him.

The posting of Montgomery to Egypt left Major General 'Ham' Roberts as the Army man responsible for remounting *Rutter* if such a decision was made. He was not keen on this without a full reappraisal of the practicalities of the operation. Montgomery had also made his opposition known. 'If another raid was mounted,' he argued, 'the objective should be anywhere but Dieppe because of German foreknowledge'.[5]

There matters seem to have stood, with *Rutter* suspended but not having been dropped and with keen support from Mountbatten and Hughes-Hallett, indifference from Leigh-Mallory and opposition by Roberts. But, as there were no other operations planned for 1942, and as Dieppe had already been sanctioned, it made sense to see if the tide and weather conditions might prove favourable for the raid to be remounted before the unpredictable weather of autumn put an end to any such enterprises.

Ultimately, the Chiefs of Staff gave their approval, and because *Rutter* had already gone through the rigorous assessment only a few weeks previously it was felt that there was no need for the reappraisal Roberts had requested.[6] But as *Rutter* had been cancelled, the new operation needed a name. It was called *Jubilee*.

Chapter 2

OPERATION *JUBILEE*

By early August 1942, the *Jubilee* plan had assumed its final shape. So far as was known, the defences of Dieppe consisted of six 5.9-inch naval guns at Varengeville-sur-Mer, the so-called 'Hess' Battery, and four 5.9-inch naval guns at Berneval, the 'Goebbels' Battery. Three field batteries, each of four guns, either 4-inch or 5.9-inch, were thought to be situated on the east headland commanding the harbour behind the town near Arques-la-Bataille, where the divisional headquarters was believed to be located, and near Appeville, not far from the fortified position of 'Quatre Vents' Farm.

DIEPPE, 19 AUGUST 1942

Showing Principal Batteries, landing places and troops engaged

RDF Station	RDF
Gun Battery (number)	4
Divisional Headquarters	DH
Officers' Mess, Pourville	OM
Aerodrome	✈
Gasworks	GW

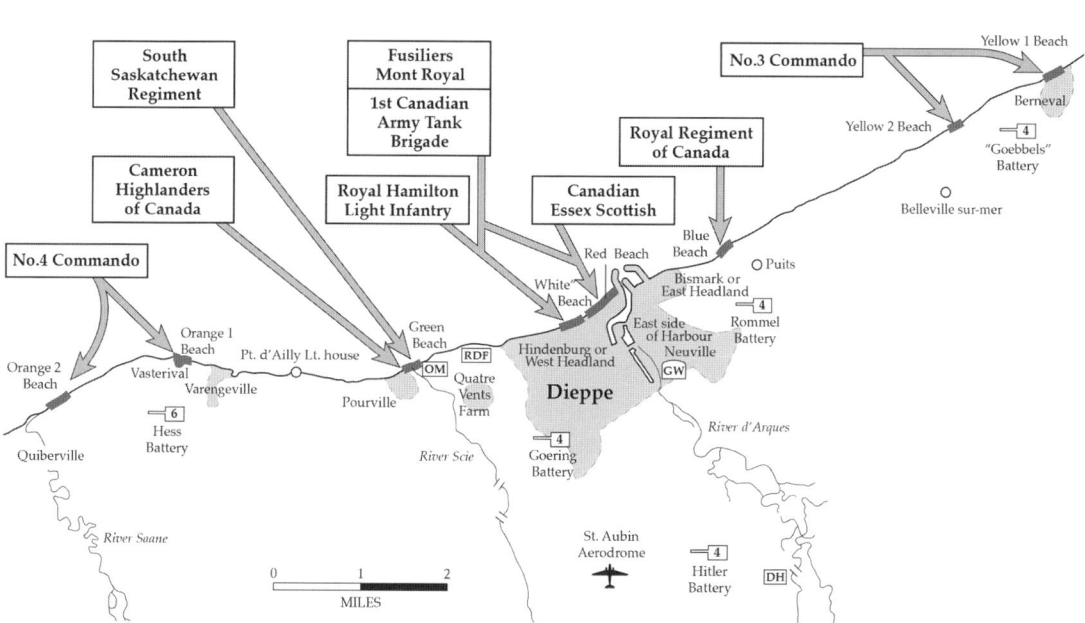

THE DIEPPE RAID

Above: Troops undergo a final training exercise prior to assault landings at Dieppe. The culmination of the training for *Rutter* and then *Jubilee* was the two Yukon exercises. The first of these, *Yukon I*, took place on the night of 11-12 June 1942. Drawing heavily on the operational plan for Operation *Rutter*, all units involved practiced their roles on a stretch of coastline at West Bay near Bridport in Dorset. This image is almost certainly from one of the *Yukon* exercises. (Department of National Defence/Library and Archives Canada)

Opposite top: A further shot of troops undertaking beach landings during what is believed to be one of the *Yukon* exercises held on the Dorset coast. The second *Yukon* exercise was held at the same location as its predecessor on 22-23 June 1942. (Department of National Defence/Library and Archives Canada)

Opposite bottom: Troops of a US Ranger battalion training somewhere in the United Kingdom. They had been attached to Combined Operations, commanded by Lord Louis Mountbatten. Training under Commando instructors, they are pictured during an exercise involving an opposed landing operation with British Naval instructors. Live ammunition and trench mortar bombs were used to create a realistic effect and prepare the men for combat conditions. (Library of Congress)

Overleaf: Canadian troops disembarking from a landing craft in July 1942 during the final exercises leading up to *Jubilee*. (Department of National Defence/Library and Archives Canada)

OPERATION *JUBILEE*

Above: A low-level aerial reconnaissance photograph of the Dieppe waterfront taken by an Army Co-operation Command aircraft a few days before the raid. (National Museum of the US Navy)

Besides these there were a number of anti-aircraft batteries, both light and heavy, some being dual purpose guns, numerous machine-guns in bunkers or pillboxes, and small guns behind concrete defences. In addition, there were eight 75mm guns in the town, emplaced so as to sweep the beaches. In fact, the defences were stronger than was thought.

The garrison of the Dieppe area was controlled by the headquarters of the 571st Infantry Regiment (equivalent to a British brigade), located on the west headland at Dieppe. It consisted of two battalions of this regiment, with headquarters on the west and east headlands respectively; a battalion of the 302nd Divisional Artillery manned the batteries mentioned above, supported by the headquarters and two companies of the 302nd Division's engineers. The remaining battalion of the 571st Infantry Regiment was in Ouville-la-Rivière, south-west of Dieppe to act as the regimental reserve.

Somewhat further afield, the Germans had large reserves. The 302nd Division's own reserve of a two-battalion infantry regiment had its headquarters at Eu, near Le Tréport, and beyond, at St. Valéry-en-Caux, was another regiment which formed the reserve of the 81st Corps in whose jurisdiction Dieppe fell.

From the transcripts of German communications, intercepted and translated at the Government Code and Cypher School at Bletchley Park, Churchill was aware that Panzer units and crack SS Divisions had been moved to the coastal zone. In particular, the 10th Panzer Division – a battle-hardened formation at full strength in both men and machines – had been moved to Amiens, less than forty miles from Dieppe. In fact, the division's nearest detachment was said to be barely nine miles south of Dieppe! Just to make matters worse, the 302nd Division, which held Dieppe, was reinforced in July and again in August to bring its strength up to three battalions totalling 3,500 men.

Little of this information was passed down to the officers responsible for conducting the raid. They were told that the town was occupied by 'low-category troops amounting to one battalion, with 500 divisional or regimental troops in support, making no more than fourteen hundred men'. The German defenders were 'second rate' and were likely to include older men aged forty to forty-five. They were not told the truth.

As for the attack itself, there were to be four flank attacks launched at nautical twilight, followed half an hour later by the assault on Dieppe. The Naval Force consisted of 237 vessels, including eight destroyers, twenty-four LCTs (Landing Craft, Tanks), seventy-four LCPs (Landing Craft, Personnel), and sixty LCAs (Landing Craft, Assault). A total of more than just over 6,000 troops would be involved, drawn from the 2nd Canadian Division, Nos. 2, 4, and 6 (Army) Commandos and 'A' Commando Royal Marines. There was also fifty men of the US 1st Rangers. As mentioned before, the RAF would deploy sixty squadron of fighters, five of bombers and two of fighter-bombers.

The principal flanking attacks were instructed to capture the 'Goebbels' and 'Hess' batteries respectively. The inner flank attacks were designed to take another battery – 'Rommel' – and attack in the rear the east headland above Dieppe.

The direct assault upon the town would see troops landed on the main beaches; they were to take and hold the town. The east and west headlands were to be heavily bombed as were also the battery on the east cliff and the two batteries behind the town and, immediately afterwards, aircraft were to throw smoke screens over the two headlands. Fighters armed with cannon were to co-operate with the attacks on the Berneval and Varengeville batteries and were also to shoot-up the defences along the sea front at Dieppe. The destroyers would provide a covering bombardment. The gunboat HMS *Locust* and other craft carrying the Marines were to enter Dieppe harbour, cut out the landing barges, trawlers and any other naval vessels, and demolish naval installations and harbour works.

The landing places were colour coded. Those to the east of Dieppe were Yellow 1 (Berneval), Yellow 2 (Belleville sur Mer) and Blue (the beach at Puits). The two landing beaches at Dieppe itself were Red (the eastern beach) and White (to the west). To the west of Dieppe, meanwhile, were Green (Pourville), Orange 1 (near Varengeville) and Orange 2 (¼ mile east of River Saâne) beaches.

As already mentioned, the attack from the Yellow beaches were aimed at the capture of the 'Goebbels' Battery, that from Orange beaches at the corresponding 'Hess' Battery. Of the inner flank attacks, that from Blue beach was designed to take another battery – 'Rommel' – and attack

THE DIEPPE RAID

Left: A final exercise is underway prior to the assault on Dieppe. Here Canadian infantrymen are embarking on landing craft during the training exercise.

in the rear the east headland above Dieppe. From Green beach, troops were to assault the fortifications at Quatre Vents Farm and take the western headland overlooking the town in the rear. Other troops were to move up the Scie Valley against the airfield at St. Aubin and the 81st Division headquarters at Arques-la-Bataille. Also from Green beach, a small team of eleven men from the South Saskatchewan Regiment were to escort a British radar expert, Flight Sergeant Jack Nissenthall, who was to enter the Pourville radar station to examine and, if possible, remove key parts of the new German Freya radar installation.

Supported by tanks those troops landed on Red and White beaches were to take and hold the town. It was intended that the landing craft would touch down while it was still dark enough to make it difficult for enemy gunners to see their targets. The east and west headlands were to be heavily bombed by RAF Douglas Boston twin-engine medium bombers, as were the battery on the east cliff and the two batteries behind the town. Immediately after their bombing run the aircraft were to throw smoke screens over the two headlands. Fighters armed with cannon were to co-operate with the attacks on the Berneval and Varengeville batteries and were also to shoot-up the defences along the front at Dieppe.

Destroyers would provide covering bombardment from distance while seaward LCFs (Landing Craft, Flak), armed with 20mm Oerlikons and 2-pounder 'pom-poms', and LCSs (Landing Craft Support), with their 3-inch and 40mm guns and 20mm cannon and machine-guns, would provide close support during the landings.

Once the defences were overcome and the troops were established in the town, the gunboat HMS *Locust* and the 'Chasseurs' (formerly French submarine-chasers or patrol craft taken over by the Royal Navy) carrying the Royal Marine Commandos were to enter Dieppe harbour, cut out the landing barges, trawlers and any other naval vessels and demolish naval installations and harbour works and, of course, collecting all the intelligence material they could gather. This included a Naval Intelligence Assault Unit of No.10 (Inter-Allied) Commando known as X Troop. Drawn from German speaking Jews or refugees, their task was the capture of a new variant of the German Enigma coding machine and associated code books believed to be housed in the German headquarters in Dieppe. This was one of the two previously-mentioned important tasks given to the raiders.

The bulk of the assaulting force was provided by the Canadian 2nd Division. It has been said that without the enthusiastic support from the Canadians *Jubilee* would not have gone ahead as no British commander would have willingly offered up his men in a frontal assault upon a well defended port. This was certainly Hughes-Hallett's opinion: 'It was hardly our [the Navy or Combined Operations] job to tell the Army how to go about their business. It was quite feasible to put them ashore on the main beaches if that's what they wanted, and our chaps said so. But my view that it was a decidedly hazardous plan was well known.'[7]

The Canadian 2nd Division consisted of the 4th Infantry Brigade, commanded by Brigadier Sherwood Lett and consisting of The Royal Regiment of Canada, The Royal Hamilton Light Infantry and The Essex Scottish Regiment; the 6th Infantry Brigade, commanded by Brigadier William Southam and consisting of Les Fusiliers Mont-Royal, The Queen's Own Cameron Highlanders of Canada and The South Saskatchewan Regiment; the 14th Canadian Army Tank Regiment (The Calgary Regiment), a unit of the 1st Army Tank Brigade equipped with Churchill tanks; light anti-aircraft and field artillery detachments (to man captured guns); and considerable numbers of engineers, plus the necessary administrative units.

Just as with *Rutter*, unfavourable weather and tides delayed the sailing of the flotilla. Then on 17 August it was reported that the forecast for the following two days, though not very good, was better than that expected later. Consequently, at 10.00 hours the necessary preliminary order was issued for the expedition to sail on the night of 18/19 August. The flank landings were timed for 04.50 hours on the 19th, the main assault for 05.20 hours.

All was set for what the Naval Commander, in a signal made before landing, termed 'an unusually complex and hazardous operation'. His words were to prove ominously accurate.

Chapter 3

WHAT DID THE GERMANS KNOW?

It is often stated the Germans had advance knowledge of Operation *Jubilee*, this being one of the reasons why it failed. Certainly, the possibility that the Germans had been forewarned of the raid on Dieppe has been examined by many historians, with some declaring that the defenders were well aware the raid was due to take place.

The most widely known of the treatise that declare the Germans were aware of the British plans is Anthony C. Brown's, *Bodyguard of Lies*.[8] He puts forward the assertion that Churchill planned that *Jubilee* would fail, by somehow intentionally informing the Germans, to extinguish insistent American and Soviet demands for a second front in 1942. The supposed reason behind this statement is that it is better to lose 5,000 men in a raid such as *Jubilee* than many times that in a premature full-scale invasion. Indeed, while he was in Moscow, Churchill told Stalin that in the Dieppe raid 'We might lose as many as 10,000 men'.[9]

Below: Two German servicemen on the western headland at Dieppe, overlooking the beach and seafront, prior to the events of 19 August 1942.

THE DIEPPE RAID

Above: German soldiers pictured in a bunker at Dieppe manning an MG 34 machine-gun, August 1942. (Bundesarchiv, Bild 101I-291-1213-34/Müller, Karl/CC-BY-SA 3.0)

Another reason which has been given for likely German foreknowledge brings in the possible Allied use of deception. In a theory put forward by Brian Loring Villa, the mounting of the raid was leaked as part of a deception plan, to let the Germans know of the raid and then they would never suspect that it was being remounted. This is supported by Mountbatten's post-war comments to the same effect.

The security and intelligence expert Nigel West reluctantly admits that the operation might have been inadvertently given away for deception purposes. He asks, 'did someone decide to capitalise

Opposite: A photograph of Willi Jakobs, who fought at Dieppe during the Allied raid in August 1942. An accompanying letter, dated July 1965, states that Jakobs (a greengrocer in Bensberg, near Cologne, at the time of writing) was a 'platoon leader when the "English" landed – most of his platoon came from Graz in Austria'.

THE DIEPPE RAID

Main image: A photograph of the seafront at Dieppe that was posted home in the war by Willi Jakobs. This is the view looking east from the western headland over the main beach (Red and White beaches during the attack) towards the harbour entrance. The distinctive form of the Casino can be seen in the centre foreground.

WHAT DID THE GERMANS KNOW?

on an abandoned plan by feeding details of *Rutter* to the enemy through a double agent, only to be caught by the reinstatement of *Jubilee*?'[10]

What is far more believable are the contents of a report by the German Commander-in-Chief, West, Generalfeldmarschall Gerd von Rundstedt.[11] It reads in part as follows: 'From middle of June, the results of photographic and visual reconnaissance of Air Squadron 3 and information from Agents collected by Headquarters revealed the concentration of numerous small landing craft on the South Coast of England … Headquarters considered the situation was such that an operation by the enemy on a large scale would certainly take place at some time at some part of the coast.'

It was also the case that the Germans knew that British leaders were under pressure from the Kremlin to mount some form of operation to help ease the situation on the Eastern Front, especially as the Germans had resumed their offensive against the Soviets in June. Indeed, all that the Germans had to do was read the Allied press.

The General Officer in Charge of the Fifteenth Army, Generaloberst Curt Haase, issued a warning of this in a special Order of the Day on 10 August. In part, this read: 'The information in our hands makes it clear that the Anglo-Americans will be forced, in spite of themselves, by the wretched predicament of the Russians to undertake some operation in the West in the near future.'[12]

In expectation of attacks by the Allies, therefore, special precautions were prescribed for coastal regions in France for periods when moon and tide were particularly favourable for landings. As early as 20 July, Hasse issued an order calling attention to three such periods: 27 July through to 3 August, 10-19 August, and 25 August up to 1 September. Accordingly, on 8 August the headquarters of the 302nd Division ordered a state of 'threatening danger' for the ten nights from 10/11 August through to that of 19/20.

Von Rundstedt also stated that the weather conditions, tides, and force of the wind were carefully observed each day and communicated to the troops. He added that on 18 August the weather forecast for the Channel area for the coming night revealed that there would be light winds chiefly from the south, but a morning mist would give decreased visibility and there would be a ceiling of low cloud. The Luftwaffe commander in the area believed that this forecast would mean that air activity was unlikely and he granted many of his pilots extended leave until midday on 19 August.

High water at Dieppe on 19 August was 04.03 hours, an ideal time for a landing. These conditions made an enemy landing appear possible and the 4th Flotilla of E-boats stationed at Boulogne was ordered to be ready to move at a half hours' notice from midnight onwards.

So, to a degree, it was true that the Germans had a pretty good idea that the British were planning a large raid, with the port of Dieppe a distinct possibility. It is interesting to note that von Rundstedt refers to 'information furnished by Agents' which indicates that there might well have been some truth in the claims made by Villa and West. But, as the General stated, such information could not be verified.

Nevertheless, there is little doubt, that when the first shots of Operation *Jubilee* rang out that misty morning in August 1942, it might have been a shock to the Germans in Dieppe, but it was certainly no surprise.

Chapter 4

YELLOW BEACH

The *Jubilee* armada sailed from England's South Coast at the end of a warm and sunny late summer's day. In an effort to avoid alerting the enemy, it was to form up in the Channel as if it was a normal convoy of civilian vessels. Strict radio silence was to be enforced until the troops actually began landing on Red and White beaches. Only shaded stern lights were to be displayed.

Between them, the various warships, landing craft and other vessels carried 298 officers and 4,663 enlisted men of the Canadian Army, approximately 1,000 officers and other ranks of Nos. 3 and 4 Commandos and the Royal Marine Commandos, eighteen members of No.10 (Inter-Allied) Commando, fifty US Rangers and a handful of other, more clandestine, individuals, making a total of 6,086 men of all ranks.

As the flotilla approached the French coast another group of vessels was also heading towards Dieppe. A German convoy of five small freighters escorted by three minesweepers or armed trawlers was making its way down the Channel from Boulogne towards Dieppe; it was on collision course with the raiders.

At 03.47 hours the inevitable happened, and as the German convoy made contact, a star shell exploded high above the most easterly group of the invasion force, Group 5. Gunfire soon blazed out across the water.

Three minutes later the Port Commandant at Dieppe was informed that the German convoy had engaged enemy ships.

Group 5 consisted of twenty-three LCPs, also known as Eurekas or R boats, that were carrying No.3 Commando, whose task it was to assault the Berneval battery in what was codenamed Operation *Flodden*. They were escorted by a steam gunboat, a motor launch, and an LCF. Sub-Lieutenant D.J. Lewis RCNVR was on the Eureka closest to the enemy when the fight began: 'A starshell went up on the starboard hand and lit the whole fleet in a horrible quivering semi-daylight. Our boat was leading the starboard [*sic*; port] column. It was immediately enveloped in the hottest tracer fire I have ever seen. The air was filled with the whine of ricochets and the bangs of exploding shells.'[13]

Outnumbered and outgunned, and with no means of illuminating the enemy vessels, the Allied boats were severely handicapped. In the encounter the British escort vessels were seriously damaged and one of the German boats was a total loss. But, more importantly, the landing craft carrying No.3 Commando along with a contingent of US Army Rangers were completely scattered, some of them being damaged.

Though Lieutenant Colonel John Durnford-Slater, already a seasoned, battle-hardened Commando, had orders that if any of his LCPs were sunk, he was to carry out his 'allotted tasks with reduced numbers', he had no idea where most of his boats had gone. He decided that a daylight assault on a well-defended position with the few boats still with the group was impracticable and

THE DIEPPE RAID

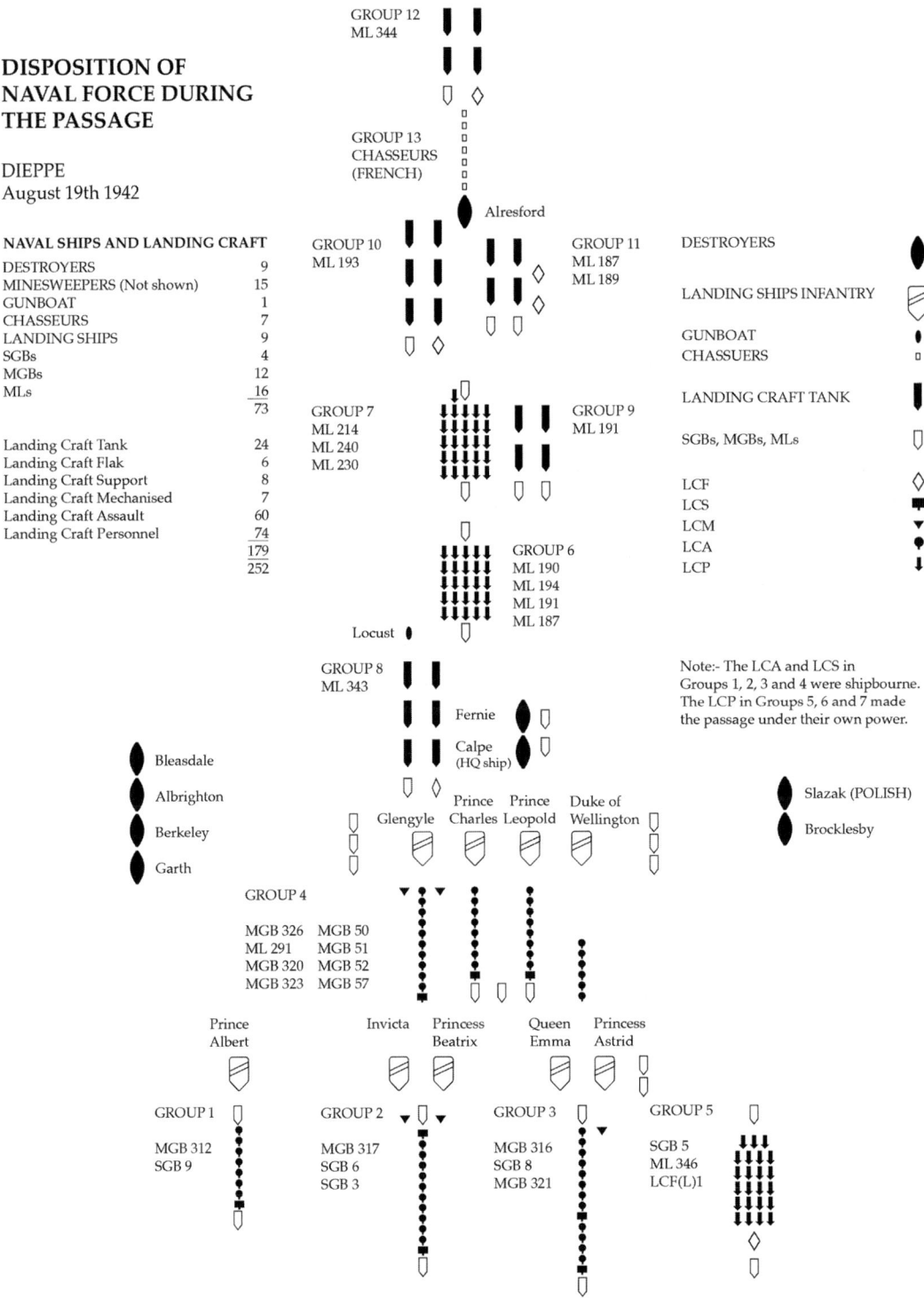

Above: An Allied warship underway off the French coast is pictured putting down a smoke screen as the Dieppe Raid gets underway, 19 August 1942. Some of the landing craft are visible.

he relayed this to General Roberts on the headquarters ship off Dieppe. It was agreed to abandon Operation *Flodden*.

Unaware that their part in the landings had been called off, the Commandos on eight of the landing craft pressed on towards the French coast determined to carry on with their mission against the Goebbels Battery. The rest of Group 5, meanwhile, turned around and headed back to England. This was just the first of the many disasters that were to be played out that fateful day.

The engagement in the Channel did not, surprisingly in view of all the alerts that the German commanders along the coast had received, raise any immediate concerns, other than at Berneval, where its defensive positions were fully manned by its garrison within ten minutes of the first shots out at sea being fired.

Goebbels Battery was situated to the north of Berneval-le-Grand. As an independent *Stützpunkt*, or strongpoint, it was separate from Dieppe and its environs and was in fact still under construction at the time of the raid. The garrison of the battery was provided by 2 Troop, 770 Army Coastal

THE DIEPPE RAID

Left: A group of Free French Commandoes pictured on the parade ground at Wellington Barracks, London. Among those who landed on the Yellow beaches were five men of the fifteen-strong French detachment of No.10 (Inter-Allied) Commando. Most of these men chose to wear their blue Marine uniforms and their 'France' shoulder insignia. (National Museum of the US Navy)

Defence Artillery Battery, who manned an observation post on the cliff edge, a command post, ammunition store, and three 170mm and four 105mm guns, all within a wired compound. A field picket, or guard post, was located on the cliffs, in a defensive position, above the entrances to the two narrow gorges leading down to Yellow Beach 1. One 20mm anti-aircraft gun was in a pillbox situated on the cliffs between Yellow 1 and 2, while pillboxes and machine-gun posts were also situated overlooking Yellow 1. The gorges were strewn with dense barbed wire entanglements, booby traps, and, in the case of the western defile, anti-personnel mines.

The first troops to land on either of the Yellow beaches were part of a detachment of No.3 Commando under Major Peter Young, whose men were landed dry shod on Yellow Beach 2 as their landing craft beached on the high tide five minutes ahead of schedule. Though Young had just two other officers and seventeen Commandos with him, he was determined to carry out the attack on the 'Goebbels' Battery as planned.

Their first task was to climb the steep cliffs to where the battery was located. They made their way quickly across the beach to where Young had spotted a gulley that led up the cliffs. Dawn was breaking as they clambered over the cliff top to find, much to their relief, the defensive posts at the head of the gulley unmanned.

The main guns of the German battery had begun firing on the main assault force heading for Dieppe and Young knew it was vitally important that he tried to silence the guns with the tiny force he had with him. He was aware that it would be futile to try and assault the battery with his depleted force and that the best he could do was to harass the battery as much as possible and to prevent it from inflicting serious damage.

When they reached the village of Berneval they tried to set up firing positions overlooking the battery. They considered setting up a Bren gun in the bell tower of the church but found that it did not have a staircase. Some of the locals suggested that the Commandos went through an orchard to a cornfield where they would have a clear line of sight to the battery. This they did and managed to get to a position within 200 yards of the battery. 'We now opened a hot fire at the smoke and flashes around the gun positions,' Young later reported. 'Groups of riflemen were firing at us from the battery position, but they were not marksmen.

'We had to fire from the kneeling position because of the height of the corn, taking snapshots and moving about, so as to offer the most difficult target to the enemy … It was harassing fire, more or less controlled. The guns were twenty or thirty yards apart and surrounded by concrete walls.'

The German guns did try to shell the Commandos, but without success, as Young explained: 'We were far too close to them so they could not depress the gun sufficiently to hit us – or anyone within a mile of us – but while they were firing at us they were not firing at the offshore shipping. They must have fired half a dozen shells into the countryside before they realised they were wasting their time and gave up. So, we had no problems at all until we began to run out of ammunition.'[14]

Also unaware that *Flodden* had been called off, a further six boats[15] reached Yellow Beach 1 under covering fire from the motor launch *ML 346*. The boats touched down at 05.10 hours, twenty minutes late. Initially unchallenged by the enemy, they soon they came under heavy fire from the cliff top ahead.

Among those who landed were the men the from the 1st US Ranger Battalion. In so doing, they became the first American troops to set foot on mainland Europe in the Second World War. One of their number, 2nd Lieutenant Edward Loustalot, had the unlooked-for distinction of being the first American soldier to be killed on European soil in the Second World War. He was shot during an attempt to silence an enemy machine-gun.

About thirty-five minutes after the first boat had reached Yellow 1, the last one arrived. This brought the number of men who landed on this beach to 120. But, as the boat pulled away from the beach, it was sunk by enemy gunfire.

The first of those ashore, led by Captain Richard Wills, pushed on as far as Berneval-le-Grand where they encountered further stiff resistance. Though the Commandos did advance about half a kilometre inland, almost level with the Goebbels Battery, and succeeded in knocking out one German machine-gun position, the odds were stacked against them. Not only did the defenders outnumber the small force put ashore, but they were soon reinforced by the equivalent of three more companies from the 302nd Division's anti-tank and reconnaissance battalion. Further German troops appeared in the form of an anti-tank company of the 570th Infantry Regiment and combat engineers from the 302nd Engineer Regiment. The Commandos and Rangers were outnumbered more than four to one.

The Commandos did receive help from the RAF, when, a little after 05.00 hours, fighter-bombers strafed the battery and later smoke bombs were dropped on the area. Some buildings were set on fire and one magazine exploded. The RAF kept up these attacks for the next four hours.

It was very evident that there was no chance of taking the battery. Consequently, at 07.00 hours it was decided to abandon the attack upon the battery and try and save as many men as possible. The commandos raced back to the beach only to find the sea empty. Having had no communication with the Commandos, it was thought that they had all perished and none of the LCPs returned to Yellow 1.

The stranded raiders came under fire from the cliffs above and were taking heavy casualties. Twenty or so took refuge in a cave where they were safe for a while, though acutely conscious that the Germans would soon be upon them. A Captain Hillems tried to swim out to a drifting and abandoned LCP, with the intention of bringing it in, but was shot in the attempt.

By 10.00 hours the Germans were on the beach and advancing down it, taking prisoners. Having no more ammunition, the senior officer in the cave ordered the men to break their weapons and

THE DIEPPE RAID

surrender. Two officers and eighty men were taken prisoner, many of whom were wounded. All the men who had landed on Yellow 1 had been killed or captured apart from two who had managed to swim out to reach boats and were saved.

With their persistent firing, Young's men on Yellow 2 had prevented the guns of the Goebbels Battery from engaging the main Dieppe anchorage from 05.10 hours until 07.45 hours, i.e. the critical phase of the assault landing. But now they had to make good their escape.

Firstly, Young sent Captain John Selwyn to see if an LCP was waiting for them. Selwyn signalled by Very light the welcome news that a boat was there, and the rest of the Commandos began a hurried fighting withdrawal, soon pursued by the Germans who fired upon them from the cliff top. Remarkably, all the men that had landed on Yellow 2 were taken off the beach, with just one man wounded by a mine.

After the raid, Hughes-Hallett wrote that the actions of Young and his men helped avert 'the exceedingly serious consequences' which might have resulted from the failure of the Yellow Beach landings. 'In my judgement,' he added, 'this was perhaps the most outstanding incident of the operation'. Young and the Royal Navy officer who had landed and recovered the Commandos, Lieutenant A.T. Buckee, were awarded the DSO.

Below: The grave of 2nd Lieutenant Edward Vincent Loustalot. Originally buried by the Germans at Dieppe, his body was moved after the war to Ardennes American Cemetery, Belgium. Two other Rangers died at Dieppe: Lieutenant Joseph Randall and Technician Fourth Grade Howard Henry. (Courtesy of Rich Peterson)

Chapter 5

ORANGE BEACH

Over to the west of Dieppe, the other large coastal battery, 'Hess' Battery near Varengeville-sur-Mer, was the target of No.4 Commando in Operation *Cauldron*. As with the Goebbels Battery, the one near Varengeville was also an independent *Stützpunkt*, with six 150mm guns in a concrete emplacement just over half-a-mile inland from the coastal cliffs. Intelligence reports had estimated there were around 200 men at the battery, with a further two infantry companies in support nearby. The emplacement was surrounded by concrete defences, landmines, concealed defensive machine-gun posts and layers of barbed wire, and was also protected from air attack by an anti-aircraft gun emplacement. On the heights between the River Saâne and Sainte Marguerite was the Quiberville-East defensive position where three companies and a heavy machine-gun section of the 571 Infantry Regiment were stationed.

Below: A plan of the attack on the 'Hess' Battery under Operation *Cauldron*.

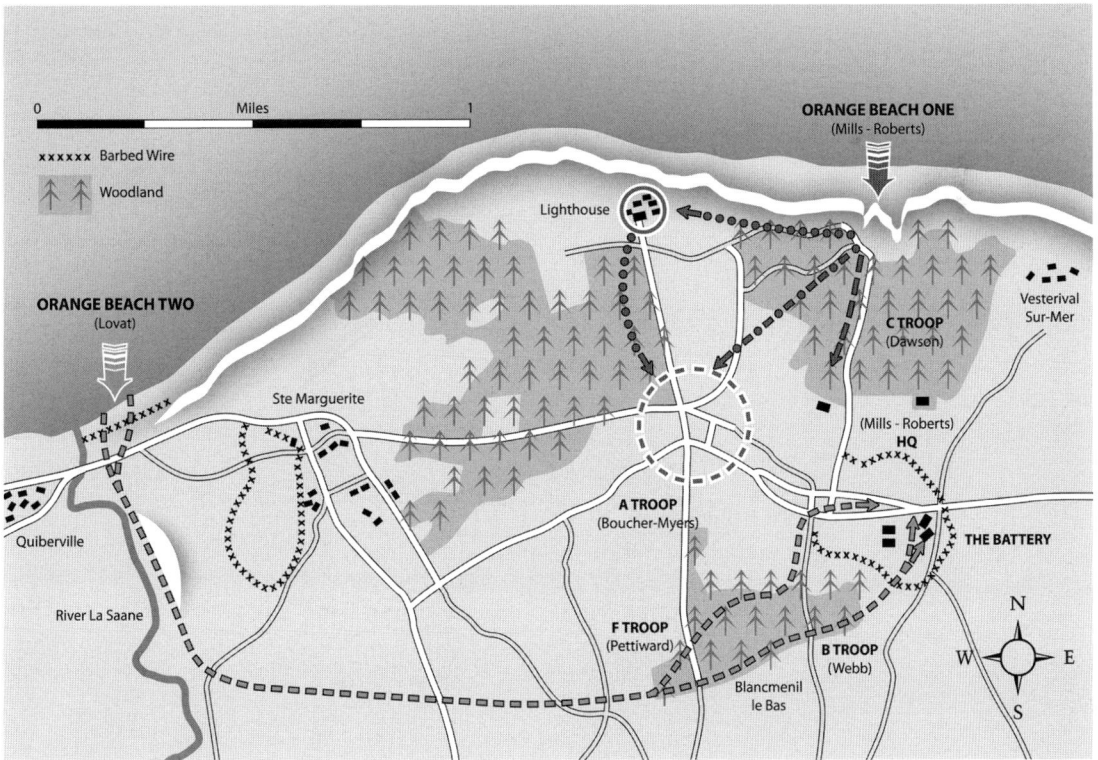

THE DIEPPE RAID

Above: Taken by Captain A.D.C. Smith, Intelligence Corps, this image shows a landing craft carrying personnel of No.4 Commando running in to land at Vasterival near Varengeville-sur-Mer. This short stretch of the French coast was Orange 1 beach on 19 August 1942.

Below: The attack on the 'Hess' Battery at Varengeville-sur-Mer complete, the men of No.4 Commando withdraw by landing craft from the Orange I beach at Vasterival under a smoke screen.

No.4 Commando was led by Acting Lieutenant Colonel Lord Lovat with a small force of 252 men. The orders Lovat had received were straightforward: Take the battery 'with all possible speed'.

Lovat's plan was a simple as his orders had been. He intended to split his Commando into two groups to land on Orange 1 and 2. Group 1 was to engage the battery positions from the front with mortars, light machine-guns and small arms fire, while Group 2 would make a wide sweep to a position behind the battery and, on a prearranged signal, assault the battery from the rear.

Speed was a vital factor in Lovat's scheme and the men were dressed in 'Skeleton Order' – just denim slacks, cardigans, rubber soled boots and stocking caps. There were to be no steel helmets, rations or water bottles to slow them down, the men carrying only a basic pouch. Faces and hands were camouflaged brown, while those of snipers were to be green. Snipers were also to use camouflage nets and telescopic sights on their rifles.

Unlike those of No.3 Commando, the landing craft taking Lovat's men into the shore encountered no problems during the passage across the Channel. Having met no opposition, the eighty-eight strong party under Major Derek Mills-Roberts reached Orange 1 exactly on time at 04.30 hours. Blowing apart the wire which defended one of the gullies that ran up the cliff, Mills-Roberts' team scrambled up the gulley where a sub-section of 'C' Troop formed a defensive perimeter around this important avenue of retreat while the remainder of Mills-Roberts's men headed off towards the battery.

Mill-Roberts knew he had to be in position to engage the battery and distract its defenders at 06.15 hours, by which time Lord Lovett would have moved round to the flank of the battery ready to mount his attack with the rest of the force fifteen minutes later, at 06.30 hours. Two minutes prior to that, at 06.28 hours, fighter aircraft were to strafe the battery and its defences.

So tight were these deadlines, that Mill-Roberts' men had abandoned any thought of stealth and they had to race towards the battery. As they rushed through the undergrowth the battery opened fire with a 'deafening' roar from its six big guns.

'We topped a little rise and came face to face with the battery,' Mill-Roberts later wrote. 'We worked our way forward to a patch of scrub, some fifty yards in front of the wood and about a hundred yards from the perimeter wire.'[16]

From there they opened fire on the surprised German artillerymen manning the nearest gun. With Mills-Roberts were two US Rangers, Sergeant Alex Szima and Corporal Franklin M. 'Zip' Koons, the latter becoming the first American soldier to kill a German in the war. For this, Koons was later awarded the British Military Medal.

The accurate rifle fire, along with that from a number of Bren guns, soon silenced three out of the four German heavy machine-gun positions in front of the battery. An anti-aircraft gun situated on the forward slope of the battery complex was also targeted and put out of action, with three successive gun crews being killed. Though the 2-inch mortar was slow coming into action, the mortar section of Troop Sergeant Major Dunning, Private Dale and Private Horn dropped their second bomb in the middle of the cordite charges and shells stacked alongside the guns ready for use, causing a huge explosion and fire. The flames spread to other powder magazines which also exploded, severely burning some of the gun crews – many of whom were shot and killed as they tried to extinguish the blaze. The battery did not fire again.

It was by then 06.07 hours – well ahead of time. Mill-Roberts knew his men had to keep up their harassing fire for another twenty minutes or more. A fierce fire-fight then developed between the Commandos and the garrison of the battery, the latter replying with rifle and mortar fire.

During this gun battle, Ranger Sergeant Szima had a very close shave: 'A sniper took the hat off my head – put a hole through the stocking cap – put a bullet through the troop sergeant-major and

THE DIEPPE RAID

Right and below: Routes up from the shore at Orange 1 beach at Vasterival, near Varengeville-sur-Mer, that were designated to be used by Major Derek Mills-Robert's force during Operation *Cauldron*. (Image right Courtesy of Tommy Larey/ Shutterstock)

THE DIEPPE RAID

Above: A wartime drawing depicting the attack on the 'Hess' Battery, and more specifically the landings at Vasterival, underway on 19 August 1942.

Opposite page top: The remains of one of the bunkers of 'Hess' Battery attacked on 19 August 1942. A German report on the attack includes the following account: 'All round there are arrangements for defending against close attack, which, however, were only lightly manned, as not enough men were available. The battery was employed against naval objectives. Fighter planes attacked it, swooping down and igniting the cartridges of nearly all the guns with small incendiary bombs. The personnel had to extinguish these fires. At the same time the enemy attacked from both sides with about 150 men. The battery crew fought gallantly; the attack lasted nearly two hours, until the battery had to surrender. The guns still intact continued firing to the end at 200 metres range … The guns have been damaged by explosive charges.'

Opposite page bottom: Another view of one of the destroyed bunkers of 'Hess' Battery at Varengeville-sur-Mer.

killed the aid man who came to help him by putting one through his head. By the time I took cover in a manure pile there were already three additional people on the ground. So this was no fooling around, and at that point I would say I was afraid.'[17]

At 06.25 hours, the Commandos 'deluged' the battery area with smoke bombs from their two mortars as, right on time three minutes later, a squadron of RAF fighters swept in to hammer the German defences. Everything had gone remarkably well up to this point. But what of Lovat with the main assault force? Mills-Roberts looked to the sky – there they were, three white Very flares meaning Lovat was in position! That was the signal for Mill-Roberts' team to head back to the defensive perimeter set up round

ORANGE BEACH

THE DIEPPE RAID

Above: A German prisoner, Unteroffizier Leo Marsiniak, is escorted ashore at Newhaven on 19 August 1942. He was captured by the men of No.4 Commando at the 'Hess' Battery at Varengeville-sur-Mer. One German report notes that 'it seems that two men of the battery were taken prisoner, but it is doubtful whether they were taken on board the enemy's ships'. The Commando Veterans Association website lists three other men returned to the UK by the men involved in Operation *Cauldron*: Bronislaw Wesierski, Max Kussowski, and Otto Samuelowitch.

Above: A US Ranger, Sergeant Alex Szima, receives a light for his cigarette at Newhaven on his return from Dieppe. Szima is possibly one of the Rangers who participated in the attack on the 'Hess' Battery. Other Allied personnel involved in Operation *Cauldron* included three Free French soldiers, two Canadian signallers of the South Saskatchewan Regiment (who landed on Orange 1 beach with 'C' Troop and were to act as liaison with the main Canadian forces in action), and three men from the GHQ Liaison Regiment, known as Phantom, who also went ashore at Orange 1 beach.

THE DIEPPE RAID

ORANGE BEACH

the head of the gully for that was No.3 Commandos' only route back to the beach.

The first wave of Lovat's Group 2 had landed nearly a mile away at Orange 2 beach, right on H-Hour. This was despite the fact that their approach had been spotted by the Germans who sent up star shells and then opened fire on the boats from an outpost on the nearby cliffs as the men began leaping onto the beach. With the first Commandos to land were two other Rangers, Staff Sergeant Kenneth D. Stempson and Corporal William R. Brady. In his after-action report, Brady explained the landing procedure for the first Section ashore: 'The 1st man that landed had the Scaling Ladder (all three sections), 2nd man had Bangalore torpedoes, 3rd man was a scout, 4th man was a Platoon Sergeant and I was the fifth man with 6 grenades'.[18] Laying chicken wire over the barbed-wire on top of the seawall, they climbed over, dropping down onto the road that ran west to Quiberville and Sainte Marguerite.

A few moments later the main body reached the beach, suffering casualties from a German mortar before they could get clear of the beach. Once formed up, Lovat's men moved quickly along the Saâne; conscious of the tight deadline they had to meet they ran all the way.

They advanced by the side of the river for about 1,600 yards before turning inland and swinging round towards the wood behind the battery. When they reached the wood, 'B' and 'F' troops divided, and Force HQ moved to the edge of an orchard near the Battery's perimeter wire. 'F' Troop was moving through an orchard to the village of Le Haut when it surprised a large group of Germans that was forming up to counter-attack Mill-Roberts' team. The Germans were killed to a man.

Left: Some of Lovat's men of No.4 Commando (Lovat Scouts), pictured at Newhaven Harbour on their return from Dieppe on 19 August 1942.

By 06.25 hours, the two assault troops were in position ready to attack, having placed Bangalore torpedoes under the perimeter wire. Three Very flares were fired into the sky. The fighters swooped over the cliff in their strafing run. The time had come.

Lovat gave the signal. 'B' and 'F' Troops then ran forward with fixed bayonets. 'It was a stupendous charge which went in,' Lovat himself later recalled, made 'in many cases over open ground swept by machine-gun fire, through a barbed wire entanglement, over running strongpoints and finally ending on the gun sites themselves, where all crews were bombed and bayoneted into submission.'[19]

Though the Germans were taken by surprise, 'F' Troop suffered heavy casualties. It was amid the chaos and the killing that the actions of one man stood out above all the brave Commandos. Captain (Temporary Major) Pat Porteous was the liaison officer between 'B' and 'F' Troops. His performance that morning was recorded in his subsequent citation for the Victoria Cross:

'In the initial assault Major Porteous, working with the smaller of the two detachments, was shot at close range through the hand, the bullet passing through his palm and entering his upper arm. Undaunted, Major Porteous closed with his assailant, succeeded in disarming him and killed him with his own bayonet thereby saving the life of a British Sergeant on whom the German had turned his aim.

'In the meantime, the larger detachment was held up, and the officer leading this detachment was killed and the Troop Sergeant-Major fell seriously wounded. Almost immediately afterwards the only other officer of the detachment was also killed.

'Major Porteous, without hesitation and in the face of a withering fire, dashed across the open ground to take over the command of this detachment. Rallying them, he led them in a charge which carried the German position at the point of the bayonet, and was severely wounded for the second time. Though shot through the thigh he continued to the final objective where he eventually collapsed from loss of blood after the last of the guns had been destroyed.'[20]

It was Commando assault engineers who destroyed the guns by backing explosive charges in the breeches and muzzles, the ends of the barrels splitting apart 'like bananas'. Instruments and most of the subterranean stores and ammunition dumps were also blown up. Considerable numbers of Germans who had hidden in underground tunnels and outbuildings, were either bayoneted or shot at close range by submachine-guns. Two officers, including the garrison commander, were also killed.[21]

It was said that the gun emplacements afterwards were a shocking sight. Dead Germans were piled high up behind the sandbag breastworks which surrounded the guns. Many of them had been badly burned when the magazine had been set on fire from the 'lucky' mortar strike. Bodies of men who had been shot by 'C' and 'A' Troops lay in and out of bunkers, slit trenches, or buildings.[22]

Twelve men from No.3 Commando were killed, a further twenty-one wounded and thirteen reported missing. Those who had been killed were left where they fell, as were some of the more seriously wounded. A medical orderly, Private Joe Pascale, courageously volunteered to stay behind to care for them in the full knowledge that he would become a prisoner. The other wounded were assisted or made their own way to the beach.

Left: Lieutenant-Colonel the Lord Lovat, Commander No.4 Commando, his trusty hunting rifle slung across his shoulder, talking to Brigadier Robert Laycock at Newhaven. Having commanded the Middle East Commando from August 1941 to August 1942, Laycock had only recently returned to Britain and, promoted to Brigadier, been handed command of the Special Service Brigade, which organised and trained all Commandos in the United Kingdom.

The tide was ebbing, and the men had to wade out to the waiting boats, with 'C' Troop, forming the rear-guard, being the last to withdraw. This was done by using light machine-guns in pairs leap-frogging one another while the rear elements put up a smoke screen. Haversacks containing smoke generators had been dumped for this purpose by the troop at the top of the gully on its way up. Smoke was also used to cover the withdrawal and no further casualties were incurred.

As the boats pulled away, the triumphant Lovat could not resist a call to Mountbatten: 'Hess battery destroyed, all enemy gun crew finished off with the bayonet – is this okay with you?'

In what has been called a 'classic' Commando action, Lovat had achieved all his objectives and he was rightfully proud of what had been achieved, but what the twenty-fourth Chief of the Clan Fraser did not know was that his operation was the only truly successful one. On the other beaches, *Jubilee* had already become a catastrophic disaster.

Left: Battle worn and exhausted, some of the Commandos are pictured here at Newhaven on the morning of 20 August. (National Museum of Denmark)

Overleaf: Ranger Sergeant Franklin M. Koons shakes hands with Lord Louis Mountbatten following his investiture with the Military Medal for his actions at Dieppe. Having volunteered for the US Army in May 1941, Koons was shipped overseas to Europe in January 1942. Initially assigned duty with the US Navy to guard military installations, Koons volunteered for service with Special Forces on 1 June 1942. Five days later he was offered a trial, which he passed, and on 19 June was assigned to the 1st Ranger Battalion. He began his training under the watchful eye of British Commandoes, in the vicinity of Weymouth and Portland, on 1 July 1942. (NARA)

Chapter 6

BLUE BEACH

During the planning for what became Operation *Jubilee* Hughes-Hallett had emphasised the importance of the inner flank attack upon Puys (or Puits), as he later explained: 'It had always been realised that unless the east headland which overlooks the town and port of Dieppe was captured, the frontal assault on the town, on which the whole operation chiefly depended, would probably fail.'

Near this eastern headland at Dieppe there were numerous objectives, notably the four-gun 'Rommel' Battery, barracks, gas works and various other gun sites. Such was the importance of taking these positions, just two days before *Jubilee* sailed Hughes-Hallett sent a letter about this to Mountbatten. In this he stated that if any of the LSIs carrying the troops to land at Blue beach were sunk, the operation should be aborted. These positions were to be attacked by troops of the Royal Regiment of Canada.

Crucially, no covering bombardment was planned to support the Royal's assault. 'Surprise is the element upon which reliance is placed for the success of the landing on Green and Blue beaches

Below: Landing craft run in to the beaches at Dieppe under the cover of a smoke screen. (Department of National Defence/Library and Archives Canada; PA-113244)

THE DIEPPE RAID

Above: Personnel landing craft draw away from ML230 to start their run-in to the beaches during the raid on Dieppe. At the time of *Jubilee*, ML230 was commanded by Lieutenant H.M. Nees RNVR. (Department of National Defence/Library and Archives Canada; PA-113247)

and they will not be supported by gunfire from destroyers', it had been decreed.[23] This was to prove a disastrous decision.

In the initial discussions over *Rutter* it had been envisaged that paratroopers would be used to take the batteries at Puits, but this was never followed through. Then in the revised plan the infantry who landed at Blue beach were to begin their attack half an hour after landing, with bomber support, against the guns and heavy coastal batteries on the East headland, with the aim of neutralizing them before the main landings took place on the centre beaches. In the *Jubilee* plan the Blue beach attackers only had half an hour in total before the main assault went in to do the same task. This would mean that the guns on the Eastern headland would still be in action when the main assault on Red and White beaches began.

The narrow beach by the tiny hamlet of Puys is situated between rising cliffs with a seawall some ten to twelve feet high running between the two cliffs. At normal high-water mark the beach between the cliffs is only some seventy-five yards wide. In 1942 the seawall was topped with barbed wire. There were only two exits through the seawall from the beach and these were also heavily wired. The strongest defensive point, as far as the attackers would be concerned, was a large brick house on the left, or eastern, flank of where the Royals would land, which had been turned into a fortified strongpoint. Below it was a camouflaged, concrete bunker which had an excellent view of the landing beach with a similar bunker on the opposite slope and a third one in between them. Together, these could cover the entire length of the beach with a hail of machine-gun fire through which it would be almost impossible for men to pass.

In addition to all of this, on the right, western, flank were two other fortified houses and various infantry positions and light machine-gun posts. Further inland were mortar positions and a battery of four 105mm field howitzers ranged for indirect fire on the beach. The whole of the Puys defensive area, *Stützpunkt* Dieppe-Ost to the Germans, was surrounded with barbed-wire and prepared for all-round defence.[24] The only hope the Royals had of breaking out of the beach had gone when the decision had been made not to bomb Puys.

The Royals were to land in three waves, with three companies in the first, the remaining company and battalion headquarters in the second ten minutes later. A special force, composed mainly of three attached platoons of the Black Watch (Royal Highland Regiment) of Canada, which was to protect the Royals' left flank against enemy intrusion, made up the third wave. But things began to go badly wrong from the beginning.

The infantry landing craft were to be led to Puys beach by Lieutenant Commander W.H. Goulding in MGB 316. This was the only motor gun boat supposed to be in that area at that time. However, MGB 315 was out of position and was moving across that area from west to east as the landing craft were forming up. Spotting the silhouette of a motor gun boat in the dark, five of the landing craft followed her instead of Goulding's boat.

By the time this error had been rectified and the column finally set off for Puys it was 03.25 hours – fifteen minutes behind schedule. Conscious that dawn was rapidly approaching and that it was vitally important to land the Canadians while it was still dark, Goulding tried to make up time by increasing speed. But not all the landing craft could keep up with the MGB and six of them fell behind and lost sight of the rest of the column.

At 04.40 hours, five minutes after the Canadians were supposed to have been disembarking onto the beach, the column of boats was still two miles out. As Goulding was preparing for the final run in, the Germans fired flares over the approaches to Dieppe harbour, 'wrenching aside the cloak of dawn' and exposing the whole of the Blue beach assault force.[25]

With no aerial bombardment, the Royals only hope of success had been if they could land undiscovered in the dark and take the German positions by surprise. All that had now gone.

However well or bravely the attackers performed, from that moment on to continue was 'an act of sheer sacrificial defiance'. The entire operation should have been called off. But there was no mechanism for the various vessels to be withdrawn.

The first wave landed seventeen minutes late. The Germans were at their posts, ready and waiting.

THE DIEPPE RAID

Few men made it to the shelter of the seawall, the enfilade fire from the German bunkers cutting them down as they disembarked from the landing craft, their bodies blocking the ramps and forcing those behind to climb over their dead or dying comrades. Even fewer succeeded in crossing the stony beach. Of the approximately 250 men who landed in the first wave of nine landing craft, only a handful reached the relative sanctuary of the seawall.

Some twenty minutes behind the first wave, the second wave reached the shoreline. Rather than reinforcing the attack, these extra troops merely added to the growing list of casualties.

Representing the Canadian press, Munro was in this second wave. 'I saw the slope, leading to a stone wall littered with Royal casualties,' recalled the lanky, bespectacled, 28-year-old reporter. 'There must have been sixty or seventy of them, cut down before they had a chance to fire a shot. On no other front have I seen such carnage. It was brutal and terrible and shocked you almost to insensibility to see the piles of dead and feel the hopelessness of the attack at this point.'[26]

Below: The scene at Blue beach soon after those Allied troops who could had withdrawn; dead Canadian soldiers lie where they fell. Trapped between the beach and fortified seawall, they made easy targets for the defenders, such as those manning the bunker on the slope in the background, the firing slit of which is visible just above the German soldier's head. (Bundesarchiv, Bild 101I-291-1230-13/Meyer;Wiltberger/CC-BY-SA 3.0)

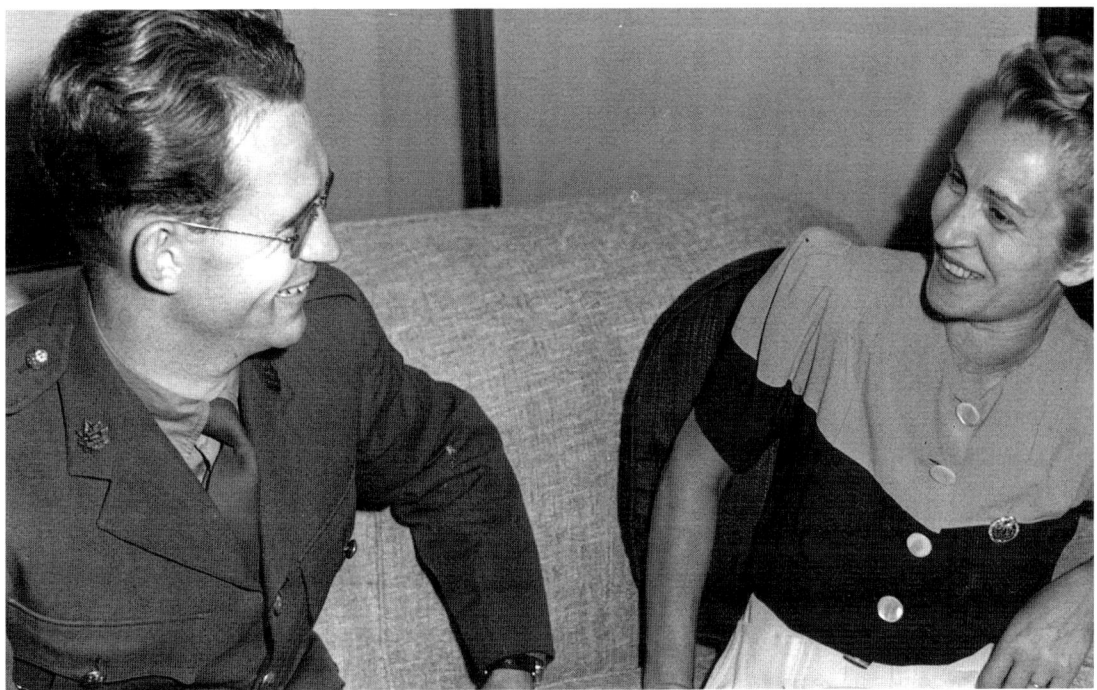

Above: War correspondent Ross Munro pictured on his return to Canada after the Dieppe Raid. He is in discussion with Mrs. W.W. Southam of Toronto. Her husband, Brigadier William Southam, was taken prisoner at Dieppe, the only officer from 6th Brigade's Headquarters to land that day. Of the raid, Munro later remarked that, 'For eight raging hours, under intense Nazi fire from dawn into a sweltering afternoon, I watched Canadian troops fight the blazing, bloody battle of Dieppe.' (Toronto Public Library)

Captain George Browne RCA, a Forward Observation Officer attached to the Royals, accompanied the Second Wave. 'In spite of the steady approach to the beach under fire, the Royals in my ALC [Assault Landing Craft] appeared cool and steady. It was their first experience under fire, and although I watched them closely, they gave no sign of alarm, although first light was broadening into dawn, and the interior of the ALC was illuminated by the many flares from the beach and the flash of the Bostons' bombs.

'The quiet steady voice of Capt. [W.B.] Thomson, seated just behind me, held the troops up to a confident and offensive spirit, although shells were whizzing over the craft, and [they] could hear the steady whisper and crackle of S.A. [small arms] fire over the top of the ALC. At the instant of touchdown, small arms fire was striking the ALC, and here there was a not unnatural split-second hesitation in the bow in leaping out onto the beach. But only a split-second. The troops got out onto the beach as fast as [in] any of the [earlier] exercises, and got across the beach to the wall and under the cliff.'

Despite what sounds like a relatively optimistic assessment, Browne was soon witnessing the death and destruction being wrought on the Royals: 'In five minutes time they were changed from an assaulting battalion on the offensive to something less than two companies on the defensive being hammered by fire which they could not locate.'[27]

THE DIEPPE RAID

Above: Bodies of many of the fallen have been brought together at the top of Blue beach. By the time the task was complete, a total of 225 of the Royals' dead lay at this spot prior to burial. (Bundesarchiv, Bild 101I-291-1230-05/Meyer; Wiltberger/CC-BY-SA 3.0)

The landing of the third wave proved equally disastrous. John 'Jack' Poolton was a member of 'D' Company's 2-inch mortar team, his haversack filled with twelve mortar bombs. 'Snipers were everywhere,' he recalled much later in life. 'It was unbelievable, unbelievable. Absolute massacre … there was smoke and there were men burning alive caught in the wire with packs on their backs, demolition packs on fire. I remember they shot one guy, our fellas, somebody shot him because he was on fire in the wire and he couldn't get out so they put a bullet in his head.'[28]

One small party of the Royals from the first wave did manage to get off the beach. This was not long after 06.00 hours. The party, numbering about twenty officers and men, was led by the Royals' commanding officer, Lieutenant Colonel Douglas Catto, in person. They cut a path through the wire at the western end of the seawall, and the colonel led them up the cliff between bursts of machine-gun fire. They cleared two houses on the clifftop, resistance being met in the first house only. The Germans then brought intense fire to bear upon the gap in the wire, and no more men got through it.

Finding itself cut off from the rest of the battalion, Catto's party moved westward above the beach in the hope of making contact with the Essex Scottish and one man who was sent forward to investigate was killed. The Essex Scottish, unfortunately, had not managed to get off the beach in front of Dieppe and Catto's men lay up in a small wood with no idea how they were going to get back to the seafront.

With this group at this point was Captain Browne. An official Canadian report describes his actions as 'one of the most remarkable individual episodes in the history of the Canadian Army Overseas so far'. As a Forward Observation Officer, Browne had the task of making contact with the Royal Navy to try and provide artillery support for the Royals after they had landed if they found the German defences too strong to be overcome. For more than two hours his wireless set was in touch with the supporting destroyer offshore, HMS *Garth*, but the Royals received little help from the navy, the message, seemingly, was not 'successfully' received by the command ship *Calpe*.[29]

After making two further attempts at reconnoitring along the cliff top to try and get in touch with any other unit, Catto decided to remain in the wood and wait for an opportunity to escape. After waiting until 16.00 hours and after all the sights and sounds of battle had faded away, Catto and his party, accepting that they were alone and completely stranded, gave themselves up at a nearby German anti-aircraft post. Though prisoners for the rest of the war, they could consider themselves among the lucky ones.

While the troops had been facing this ordeal ashore, the landing craft had been withdrawn and were lying just under a mile offshore. Those which were badly damaged or had severe casualties were ordered to move to the westward off Red and White beaches.

Shortly before 06.00 hours an LCA endeavoured to approach the beach but was hit and sunk. Soon after 07.00 hours a message was received from the shore by Hughes-Hallett on HMS *Calpe* asking for all landing craft to return to Blue beach to evacuate the infantry. Only two craft picked up this signal – LCS 8 and LCA 209, which were patrolling off the beach.

The latter went in and was half swamped by the rush of soldiers. Private E.J. Simpson was on board the landing craft: 'There was a terrible scramble and nearly everyone still alive on the beach made for the small ramp doors. The slaughter was awful. The boat had to be pushed off the beach. It was so full of holes it began to sink.' Bullets were still 'pouring' into the landing craft when, fifty yards out, it was near-missed by a heavy shell which turned it over onto its keel where it remained afloat upside down. Only two of the crew and one soldier from this craft survived.

Among the signals received by HMS *Garth* was at least one from Browne saying that Blue beach was asking for help and evacuation. The Naval Force Commander ordered Lieutenant Commander Goulding, who was onboard the destroyer *Calpe*, to take a motor launch and attempt an evacuation.

Goulding accordingly boarded ML 291 at 11.00 hours, and, as none of his own landing craft were in the vicinity, he collected some assault and support landing craft and made for the beach. Very heavy fire was opened as this improvised flotilla approached and they were forced to retire. No one had been seen alive on the beach, and Goulding signalled *Calpe* reporting failure to evacuate. Another attempt to evacuate the beach was made shortly afterwards by some of the landing craft from the former cross-Channel ferry, *Princess Astrid*. They too saw no one on the beach and retired under heavy fire with one of the landing craft being sunk.

Scarcely any of the Royals escaped from Blue Beach. Of the 556 men who set off from England, 464 were either killed or captured. With 200 of these men being killed, the regiment suffered not only the highest fatal casualty rate of any unit on the raid, but a loss rate stated to be the highest suffered by any Commonwealth or American unit, per proportion of forces engaged, during the entire war.

Chapter 7

GREEN BEACH

The combined flotilla of the former passenger-liner-turned-troopship *Princess Beatrix* and the troopship *Invicta*, previously a Southern Railways ferry, were to land officers and men of the South Saskatchewan Regiment at Pourville. The Canadians were to take the German defence headquarters there, as well as the nearby radar station and other targets. They were also to aid the Royal Hamilton Light Infantry in taking the fortified Quatre Vents Farm, the capture of which was regarded as essential if the withdrawal was to be achieved without severe casualties. This was because there were two artillery batteries there, each with four 105mm 14/19 Czech field howitzers. The attackers were also to cover the western flank of the outer perimeter of Dieppe.

The Queen's Own Cameron Highlanders of Canada were to land half an hour later and pass through to attack the airfield of St. Aubin and link up with the Calgary Regiment's tanks to take the Divisional Headquarters at Arques-la-Bataille and a heavy gun position not far away.

Pourville was within the Dieppe *Stützpunktgruppe* and, therefore, most positions were prepared for all-round defence being protected by trench systems and barbed wire entanglements, which included as many as seven machine-gun pillboxes and 40mm anti-aircraft guns. Two companies of 2 Battalion, 571 Infantry Regiment formed the bulk of the garrison in Pourville itself.

Pourvllle lies two-and-a-half miles to the west of Dieppe at the base of the River Scie which flows into the Channel near the middle of the beach. That beach, approximately 800 yards long and was about twenty-five yards wide at high tide, stretches between rising cliffs.

The South Saskatchewan Regiment, numbering 523 officers and men under Lieutenant Colonel Dollard Merritt, landed unopposed at 04.52 hours. Undetected by the enemy, they were just two minutes late, though further to the west than intended.

The plans called for 'B' Company to clear the town of the enemy, while 'A' Company mounted the eastern heights to attack the coastal batteries and the radar station. 'C' Company was to move to the south-west and destroy a German Army motor transport repair shop and several machine-gun positions on the western edge of the Scie valley. 'D' Company would follow 'A' Company to link up with the Royal Hamilton Light Infantry in its assault upon Quatre Vents Farm.

The Canadians now had to mount the seawall using scaling-ladders, the first men up using wire-cutters to cut through the barbed-wire which topped the structure. Once through the gap, those companies whose objectives lay to the east had to turn left and dash through the silent streets of Pourville to the bridge over the River Scie which led to the road leading to eastern ridge towards Dieppe. But before they could reach the bridge, the Germans awoke, quite literally, to the danger they were in.

As 'A' and 'D' companies raced for the bridge they encountered intense fire from enemy positions on the hill leading to the eastern heights on the other side of the river. In the face of this fire, the

Opposite page: Bound for Green beach, infantrymen of The Queen's Own Cameron Highlanders of Canada clamber into their landing craft for the run ashore on the morning of 19 August 1942.

Left: A portrait of Lieutenant Colonel Cecil Merritt VC. The bridge over the River Scie in Pourville, where Merritt earned the Victoria Cross, was renamed in his honour for the 50th anniversary of the raid in 1992. Merritt's VC was the first such Canadian award to be gazetted in the Second World War. (Toronto Public Library)

advance of 'A' Company ground to an abrupt halt. Some tried to storm the bridge but were beaten back, while others attempted to swim across the river, though few reached the eastern bank. Those who did could do nothing other than shelter as best they could from the enemy fire. This was a serious setback, potentially jeopardising the withdrawal of the entire force. For almost thirty minutes 'A' and 'D' companies were held up at the bridge, all the while taking heavy casualties.

Seeing how critical the situation had become, Colonel Merritt left his headquarters and walked to the bridge. He stepped forward in full view of the enemy, took off his helmet, walked on to the bridge and shouted: 'Come on, these Germans can't hit a thing – let's go!' Apparently oblivious to the enemy fire, he strolled across waving his helmet to encourage his men forward, and, amazingly, they followed him and launched their assault on the enemy-held heights.

The opposition, though, was heavy, and with increasing casualties among leaders, progress was slow. Throughout, Merritt was 'in the forefront of the bitter struggle around Pourville, exposing himself recklessly and displaying an energy almost incredible'. He personally led several successful attacks on the well-sited pillboxes from which the enemy covered the open hillside. But without artillery the heavily fortified main positions could not be breached.

After one attempt, Merritt carried a wounded officer back through machine-gun fire to relative safety. One man remembered Merritt's breath-taking composure: 'When Colonel Merritt saw us stop, he said. "What's the matter with you fellows? You're not frightened are you?" And without waiting for an answer he said, "Come out here." So I walked out in the middle of the road, with great trepidation, and he swung his helmet on the forefinger of his left hand and said, "You see? There's no fire out here."'[30]

'C' Company moved across to tackle the hill to the west, driving up through the terraces, silencing machine-gun posts as they went and carving a route for the Canadian Cameron Highlanders who were scheduled to soon make their appearance. Though 'A' and 'D' companies were struggling to survive by the banks of the Scie, 'B' Company was sweeping through the town. All the houses and hotels along the promenade were found to be empty and it was in the garage of one of those houses that Battalion Headquarters was set up, but it was not long before the Germans responded.

Following Merritt's example, many of the men of 'A' and 'D' companies had crossed the Scie by one means or another, but collectively, they were not strong enough to break through the enemy's defensive positions on the eastern slopes. It was the same to the west, where 'C' Company's progress had come to a halt.

One of the objectives of the attack at Green Beach was for Flight Sergeant Jack Nissenthall, the RAF electronics and radar expert, to break into the new German Freya radar station at Pourville. For the mission, the second of the particularly important tasks handed to the raiders, Nissenthall was attached to Captain Murray Osten's 'A' Company of the South Saskatchewans. On the raid he was to be escorted by a team to protect him but also to prevent his capture, due to his exceptional technical knowledge. The Canadians had been given very firm instructions; under no circumstances was he to fall into German hands. This was made very clear to him: 'Ten men will be delegated to help you in every way. If, however, you are wounded and you cannot be brought back to England, they will be ordered to shoot you. Also in your escape kit will be medication that will enable you to depart from the earthly scene in quick time.'[31]

Having landed with 'A' Company on the western side of Green Beach, Nissenthall's team was faced with the same problem most of the of the troops had met – that of having to cross the River Scie. Following Merritt on one of his bold strides over the bridge they reached the far bank and began to mount the hill surmounted by the Freya station.

Below: Lieutenant Colonel Cecil Merritt VC resting upon his return to England in April 1945. Having been GSO2 of the 3rd Canadian Division, in March 1942 he was promoted to command the South Saskatchewan Regiment. Two months later, they moved to the Isle of Wight to train for the Dieppe Raid. (Toronto Public Library)

THE DIEPPE RAID

Above: A group of Allied troops captured by the Germans at Dieppe are marched away into captivity. Some of the men seen here are members of the Queen's Own Cameron Highlanders of Canada. This includes Private John Michael Machuk, who can be seen in the front row, second from the right, with his hand on his stomach. Machuk was held in two German prison camps before escaping by jumping over a hedge into a ditch. While he was hiding there, a German stopped to urinate over the hedge, and onto Machuk, but didn't realize the presence of the 22-year-old Canadian.

Shell bursts and small-arms fire followed the zigzagging soldiers up the mostly open slope. There now were only about twenty-four men left of 'A' Company's original 100. Nissenthall's bodyguards were down to seven, three of whom were lightly wounded. The remaining men finally reached a point just below the top, where they stopped. At this point Nissenthall could see the Freya station on the hill above. It was a solid concrete building surrounded by a high blast wall, which, in turn, was protected with earth and sandbags. Beneath the aerial was a small cabin where the operator sat. Machine-gun posts and trenches for infantry had been dug between the Freya station and the barbed wire perimeter fence.

'A' Company alone was obviously in no shape to be able to help Nissenthall break into the Freya compound. So, along with two of his bodyguards, he ran back to Pourville and to battalion headquarters and a three-man mortar team was put together to help him.

The six men set off back towards the bridge. As they started to run across the open space in front of the casino a mortar bomb landed near the seawall and blew the party off their feet. When they recovered their senses, they saw that half of their number had been killed. A despondent Nissenthall reached 'A' Company, still determined to complete his mission.

Unbelievably, he decided to return to Pourville to enlist support one more time – and again he had to have an escort, this time with just one other courageous man. Repeating the hazardous crossing of the Scie he again reached battalion headquarters. Another mortar crew was assembled and, this time, the whole party made it safely to the remnants of 'A' Company. But this added firepower proved still too little to make an impression on the well-defended Freya site.

Time, and opportunity, was slipping away. But there was a fallback plan which had been considered before the raid. British listening centres on the South Coast had often picked up coded messages being sent between the German radar sites by radio and morse. Cryptographers in Britain then decoded these messages and thus were able to determine the capabilities and strengths of the radar stations. However, now the stations used land line telephones which could not be intercepted. If Jack could cut these lines and force the use of radio again, then the German transmissions could again be picked up in Britain, and the latest secrets revealed.

With the surviving members of 'A' Company providing covering fire, Nissenthall crawled 120 feet to the triple-mast cable support. He wedged himself between the poles and worked his way to the top. Fifteen feet above the ground, with bullets flying around him, Nissenthall pulled out his wire clippers and began cutting the eight cables. With the last one severed, he dropped to the ground and safely reached his comrades.

Almost immediately after Nissenthall had cut the Freya's telephone wires, listening posts along the Sussex coast picked up radio communications from the Pourville station. Unable to communicate through the secure land line, as hoped the German operators had resorted to using open radio. From these transmissions an enormous amount of information was gleaned. Gradually, a complete picture of the German radar network emerged. Of his small team, only Nissenthall and one other returned safely to England.

The Queen's Own Cameron Highlanders of Canada were late. The 503 officers and men were supposed to land at 05.20 hours – the same time as the main landings on Red and White beaches at Dieppe. They made their appearance at 05.50 hours, in broad daylight with the enemy unsubdued.

To add to the delay, the bulk of the Camerons, like the South Saskatchewans before them, were disembarked on the western side of the beach with the remainder deposited on the eastern side, the two parts separated by the Scie. Had the Camerons landed on schedule and in the correct place their weight of numbers, added to those of the South Saskatchewans, might have been sufficient to force a way through the German positions. But divided they fell.

One party of the Camerons, under Captain Young, which had landed on the eastern side of the Scie, found itself alone and unable to communicate with the rest of the battalion. All Young felt he could do was create as much mayhem as possible, so he moved inland along the river for some 500 yards before turning uphill. There they ran into a collection of enemy-occupied houses, described as a small village, and were held up by intense mortar fire.

On the western side of the river Major A.T. Law with the main body of the Camerons reached a similar decision as had Young and he too led his men inland along the Scie. They penetrated as far as a ridge overlooking Bas de Hautot village from where they could look down on where they were supposed to link up with the Calgary Regiment's tanks. But no tanks were to be seen.

With little hope of success, yet determined to do all he could, Law pushed on to Quatre Vents Farm. It was all to no avail. German forces in the area around the farm had been reinforced and, without the support of the tanks, the Camerons stood little chance of taking the strongpoint.

By this time, it had become all too evident to the Camerons that were not going to be able to achieve their objectives and Major Law had also pulled back to Pourville to join Merritt's South Saskatchewans. The only course of action remaining to the Canadians was to hold out until they could be evacuated.

The Germans had reached the same conclusion and saw their chance to counter-attack. They dislodged 'C' Company of the South Saskatchewans from the high ground west of Pourville which dominated both the slopes and the beach from where the withdrawal was to take place.

The request to be evacuated was sent to the command ship *Calpe* and the signal 'Vanquish from Green Beach 1000 hours' was received, indicating that evacuation would take place at that hour. The Canadians had to hold out until then. But at 09.45 hours another signal message was received stating that 'Vanquish' would not be until 11.00 hours.

There were some 200 wounded men huddled against the seawall under the care of the South Saskatchewan's medical officer, Captain Frank Hayter, who was attempting to prepare those under his care for the move down to the water's edge. Even the fifty-odd German captives were pressed into service to lay out the wounded in priority groups for the withdrawal.

Finally, the landing craft arrived, but heavy losses were incurred as the men moved over the open stretch of sand and water to the boats. Witnessing his men being killed, at about 11.30 hours, Merritt collected some men and attacked machine-guns to the west of the beach which were proving particularly deadly. He silenced the enemy guns and by midday most of the troops had been re-embarked.

Merritt formed the remainder into a rear-guard, holding off the Germans and allowing the boats to get away to safety until at about 13.30 hours, their ammunition almost exhausted. Merritt, refusing to raise a white flag, sent a German prisoner forward to invite the enemy to come forward and take the Canadians' surrender.

Though he marched off into captivity, Charles Cecil Ingersoll Merritt would later receive the award he had so patently deserved – the Victoria Cross. Jack Nissenthall, who had shown courage and determination way beyond the call of duty, received no such recognition. Because of the nature of his secret mission, it was said, no award could be granted.

Chapter 8

RED AND WHITE BEACHES

The main assault was to be delivered against the sea front of Dieppe itself. This was some 1,700 yards long backed by a sea wall, boulevards and gardens. The western end (White beach) was to be attacked by the Royal Hamilton Light Infantry, the eastern (Red beach) by the Essex Scottish Regiment, supported by the 14th Canadian Tank Battalion (The Calgary Regiment) and some small subsidiary units.

Below: An oblique aerial photograph of Dieppe which, taken in June 1945, shows the stretch of the town's seafront that was designated as Red beach on 19 August 1942. (NARA)

Above: The run-in to Dieppe – pillars of smoke rise above the town as Operation *Jubilee* unfolds on the morning of 19 August 1942. (National Museum of Denmark)

Immediate success in this sector was a cardinal feature of the plan. The Royal Hamilton Light Infantry was to attack gun positions, notably the 'Goering' heavy battery, assist the South Saskatchewan Regiment in the attack on Quatre Vents Farm and join the Essex Scottish Regiment in controlling Dieppe. The latter was to concentrate on the dock area and eastern side of the town, attack various gun sites, capture two emergency landing grounds, and join up with the Royal Regiment of Canada.

The landings were to be supported by tanks landed at White beach. Detachments of the Royal Canadian Engineers were to land with the first wave and demolish portions of the sea wall to enable the tanks to get on to the esplanade and thence to enter the town and co-operate with the Cameron Highlanders from Green beach against St. Aubin and Arques-la-Bataille. Les Fusiliers Mont-Royal was to act as floating reserve and to land later as a rear-guard to cover the withdrawal. But, as we already know, neither the Royals nor the Cameron Highlanders had been able to achieve their objectives and the operation was failing. This, though, was yet to manifest itself.

A Canadian report on the German defences noted that the defended localities were mainly concentrated on the high ground overlooking Dieppe. That said, the actual front of the town, from the Casino to the harbour mole inclusive, was held by two infantry platoons and an 'experimental' naval company. This last unit was armed with five 37mm anti-tank guns and three light machine-guns, while the infantry had one 75mm gun, one 37mm anti-tank gun, one tank (in a static position) and one 47mm anti-tank gun. There were also 'numerous' anti-aircraft guns manned by Luftwaffe personnel on both headlands – these were able to enfilade the beach and its approaches.

Above: Plumes of water thrown up in the air among the various assault and landing craft by German shellfire shortly after dawn on 19 August. (National Museum of Denmark)

The German weapon positions were set in caves in both headlands, with guns that could be brought out to fire and then pulled back in, and most of the weapons on the promenade were sited in concrete pillboxes, casemates and bunkers. The Germans had even constructed underground bunkers on the promenade covered with grass and completely invisible from the air.

Access to the beach from the promenade for pedestrians was via steps in gaps in the concrete sea wall, one about 100 yards west of the Casino and a second near the junction of Red and White beaches. This wall was about ten feet high, but the shingle had been washed up against it, and for most of its length the height above the beach varied from two to four feet. A line of barbed wire stretched the length of the beach, both in front and on top of the wall. The beach itself was composed of pebbles of an extremely hard mineral called chert. This seemingly small fact was to have a profound effect on the events that unfolded over the following few hours.

As the raiding force headed for Dieppe itself, it was spotted by a flotilla of German ships waiting off the harbour. Star shells were fired, illuminating the assault craft arranged in line closing in on the shoreline. This just served to confirm to the Germans that they were about to be attacked, the forces at Dieppe having already been alerted, as we have learned, by the naval engagement which proved so disastrous to No.3 Commando.

At 05.10 hours, ten minutes before H-Hour, the four warships of the 2nd Destroyer Division – HMS *Berkeley*, HMS *Bleasdale*, HMS *Garth*, and HMS *Albrighton* – opened fire with their 4-inch main armament on the hotels and houses along the promenade as the landing craft sped towards

THE DIEPPE RAID

Above: Another view of landing craft and other vessels taken during the run into the beaches at Dieppe. The German people first learnt about the raid through the Norwegian German Radio Service at 12.00 hours Central European Time on the 19th. A short message stated that: 'The British in the early hours of this morning made a landing on the French channel coast supported by considerable numbers of air and naval forces. The British who have landed infantry and tanks met hard and successful resistance of the German troops. Several British tanks were destroyed by German artillery fire which started immediately. German countermeasures continue according to plan.'

the beach. The Essex Scottish was carried ashore by two flotillas, each consisting of eight LCAs and one LCS(M), touching down on the pebble beach of Dieppe close to the scheduled time of 05.20 hours.

The vessels transporting the RHLI were just two minutes behind at 05.22 hours, about 200 yards east of the Casino as planned. The troops actually landed with little loss, but their troubles then developed rapidly, because instead of advancing quickly while the enemy was still taking cover from the aerial and naval bombardment, they remained under the shelter of the sea wall, thus losing precious moments. When they started to advance the Germans had recovered and opened a heavy fire.

A small band of the Royal Hamiltons, led by Captain A.C. Hill, managed to break into the town where it stormed the Casino. It was joined by a party of Royal Canadian Engineers, which blew up pillboxes nearby and used demolition charges to end all resistance in the Casino itself. The engineers also blew up, among other defensive structures, a 4-inch gun emplacement. Hill then pressed on

Right: The crew of what appears to be a PaK 38 anti-tank gun stand ready to fire near the southern end of the Rue de Sygogne in the event of a possible penetration by any of the Allied tanks or other armoured vehicles.

deeper into the town. The Hamiltons went as far as the Église Saint-Rémy, some 200 metres inland in Rue Saint-Rémy, but Hill's band was too small to hold its own unsupported and was obliged to retreat.

The murderous enfilade fire from guns concealed in the eastern cliffs was very much greater than had been anticipated. These guns were 'impossible to detect even at close range until they fired,' reported Lieutenant-Commander McMullen, and 'could not easily be silenced by our own fire. This enfilade fire made the capture and retention of the beaches almost impossible and was therefore the main cause of the failure to press on through Dieppe and attain objectives laid down in the plan.'[32]

Another factor was the vast depth of wire between the seawall and the buildings lining the far side of the promenade from where the Germans were firing directly at the attackers. Until they could get to the buildings and silence the enemy, the attackers were going to suffer more and more casualties. The men of the Essex Scottish tried to blast a way through the wire with a Bangalore torpedo, but it only cut halfway through the six-feet-deep entanglement.

A party of the Essex Scottish did penetrate into Dieppe from the beach but, as with Hall's group from the Hamiltons, there was little they could do to influence the course of the battle.

All this time covering fire was being vigorously given by support craft, but their light guns had little real effect. One of these support craft, LCF(L) 2, dared to close to point-blank range to give the best support she could. But one-by-one her guns were knocked out and her captain killed before she was sunk.

The destroyers were also heavily engaged, but their guns were too light to make much of an impression on the strong and well-concealed enemy positions. It had been intended to control the destroyers' fire by means of Forward Observation Officers who were to land with the troops, but most of them became casualties or, as we have read, could not establish communication. Nevertheless, the destroyers achieved some success, with HMS *Albrighton*, for example, silencing an anti-aircraft battery above Pourville.

In his report on *Jubilee*, Mountbatten stated: 'At no time was the support which the ships were able to give sufficient for the purpose and this is one of the main reasons why the landing at Blue, Red and White beaches was unsuccessful.' The British vessels also came under air attack from the Luftwaffe despite the very efficient protection given by RAF fighters.

General Roberts on HMS *Calpe* had only limited information on what was happening ashore and had no idea how critical the attackers' position had become. In Hughes-Hallett's words: 'The military situation was completely obscure, and the large quantities of smoke drifting inshore made it impossible to see what was happening.' What was evident, however, was that there was still no lessening in the volume of fire from the Germans. Yet Roberts still had his floating reserve in hand – Les Fusiliers Mont-Royal – and he decided to deploy it on Red Beach to make a final push to break German resistance.

With the aid of smoke, and in the face of very heavy fire, a number of the Fusiliers were successfully put ashore at 07.04 hours under the direction of Lieutenant Commander J.H. Dathan, Senior Officer of Group 7, in ML 214. He took in twenty-six LCPs, losing two when beached and a third during the withdrawal. So intense was the enemy's fire that the Fusiliers achieved little or no success and suffered serious losses as soon as they landed. Two small parties did succeed in penetrating into the town and dock area, but few returned.

Above: Two wounded Canadian soldiers lie on the beach at Dieppe. In the background can be seen the still burning TLC 5 (No.121), which transported the three Mk.III Churchills of 9 Troop, 'B' Squadron, 14th Canadian Tank Battalion (The Calgary Regiment) – *Buttercup*, *Blossom* and *Bluebell* – and one Daimler Scout car, *Harry*. Having come ashore in front of the Casino and dismounted the tanks, she was soon hit by mortar and artillery fire, leaving her blazing and beached, most her crew dead, dying or wounded. It is *Blossom* that can be seen on the right in this picture. (Bundesarchiv, Bild 101I-291-1205-14/Koll/CC-BY-SA 3.0)

THE DIEPPE RAID

Main image: A closer view of TLC 5.

THE DIEPPE RAID

Above: A Royal Navy destroyer bombarding targets ashore during Operation *Jubilee*. One of those observing the attack from a Royal Navy warship offshore was the American war correspondent Drew Middleton, an employee of the Associated Press. The following is part of an account by Middleton that was published in the *Western Daily Press*, under the title 'With the Navy at Dieppe', on 21 August 1942: 'We steamed through smoke, and in the early sunlight saw the burning houses of Dieppe, and heard the rattle of rifle fire and the clatter of machine-guns. Shells from four-inch guns of British destroyers began to whistle overhead. Watching through field glasses you could see them smash into a row of hotels once sacred to honeymooning Britons along one side of Dieppe's main boulevard. Slowly British gunners brought the hotels down around the ears of the German machine-gunners and riflemen which they sheltered. As they disintegrated under the shelling you could see the Allied troops moving forward, running and pausing to fire.'

Right: A few of the German defenders pose for the camera in the trenches they occupied during the fighting. (National Museum of Denmark)

Overleaf: The crew of a German field gun pause to enjoy a drink in the immediate aftermath of the fighting on Red and White beaches. Note the still-burning landing craft TLC 5 on the beach in the background. The battered pillbox just beyond the gun is that which was located at the top of the beach by the north-eastern corner of the Casino – which is visible on the left. (National Museum of Denmark)

THE DIEPPE RAID

Above: Three Canadian soldiers taken prisoner at Dieppe. The individual in the centre has been identified as Corporal Harold Nelson of No.2 Provost Company, Canadian Provost Corps. Provost support for the raid was provided by a forty-one-strong contingent from No.2 Provost Company under the command of Captain Edward Hammond Stevenson. Of that number, one man was killed and eighteen, including Nelson, were captured in the attack. Of those who returned to the UK, six were wounded. Despite his wounds and three years in captivity, after the war Nelson returned to Winnipeg and become a Canadian amateur heavyweight wrestling champion.

Chapter 9

TANK ATTACK

As part of the plans for *Jubilee*, it was decided that a total of thirty Churchill tanks of the 14th Canadian Army Tank Regiment (The Calgary Regiment) were to be landed in four waves on Red and White beaches. Not only was this the first unit of the Canadian Armoured Corps ever to go into battle, but also the first time the new Churchill tanks would see action.

Four types of Churchill tank were utilised at Dieppe. The Mk.I had a cast turret equipped with a 2-pounder and .303 Besa machinegun, along with a 3-inch howitzer in the hull. The Mk.IIs were the same except that a second Besa replaced the howitzer, while the Mk.II Oke variants had Ronson flamethrower apparatus added. Lastly, the Mk.IIIs had a welded turret holding the newly-developed

Below: Lieutenant Marcel Lambert's Churchill Mk.III, *Blossom* of 9 Troop, 'B' Squadron, is pictured still smouldering on the beach. As the *Windsor Star* declared, Lambert 'was listed as missing and presumed dead after the … raid, when his tank was immobilized. His five-man tank troop fought on the beach until taken prisoner nine hours after landing. Four to six weeks after his family got word that he was missing, they were informed he was in a German prison camp with about 1,800 other Commonwealth officers. He spent three years there.'

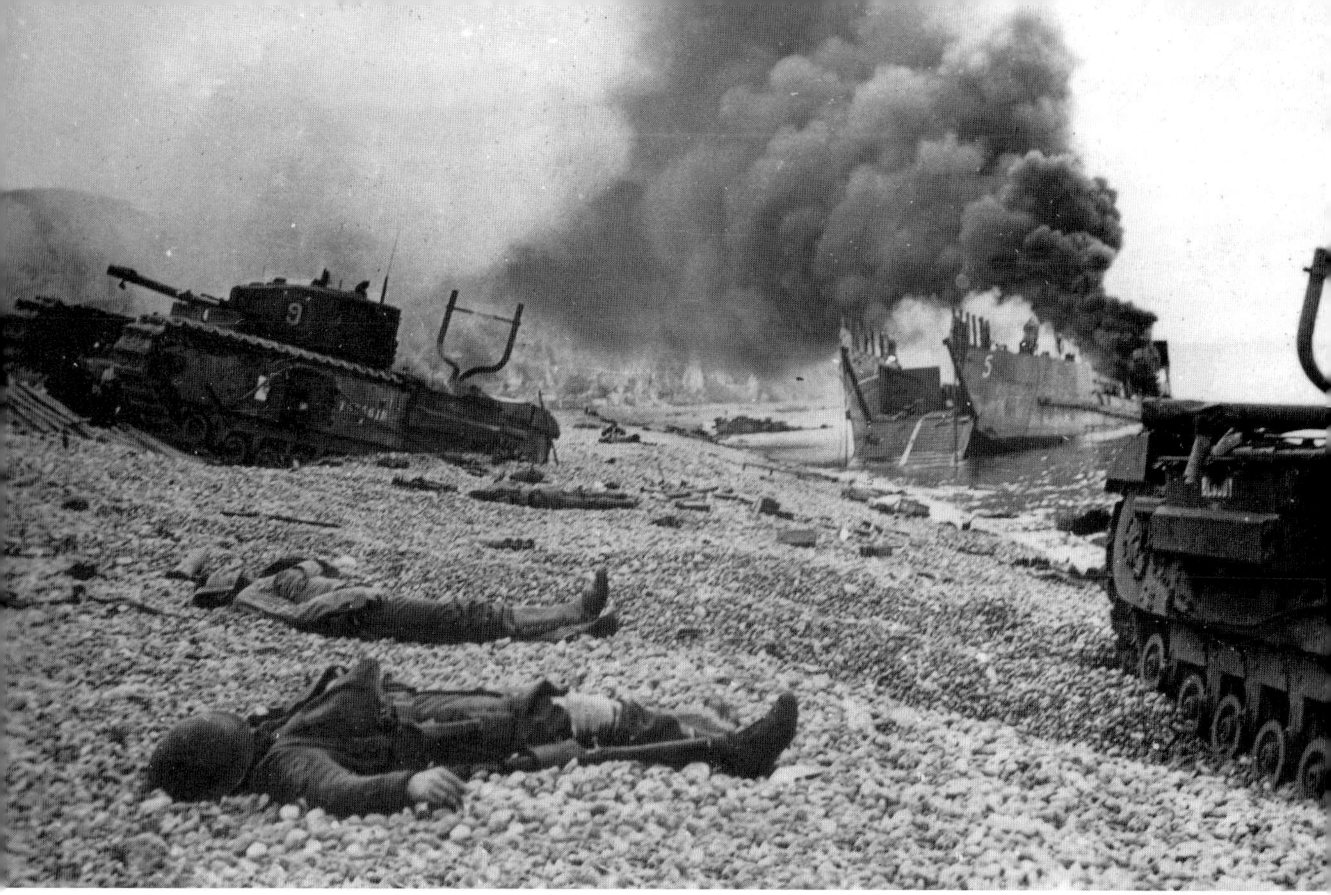
9
5

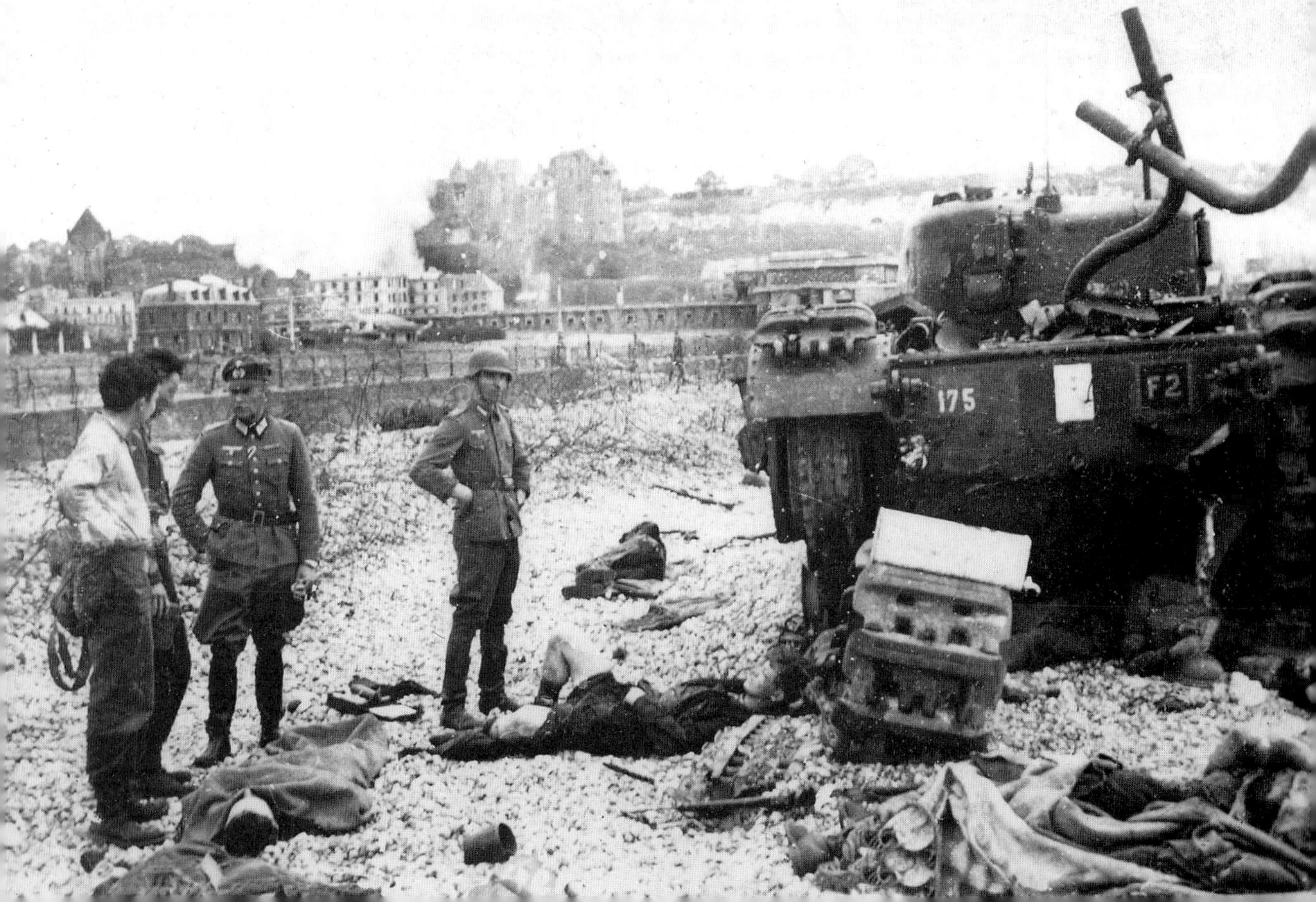
175
F2

Opposite top: *Blossom* can also be seen on the left in this view of the beach at Dieppe. The tank in the right foreground is Mk.III T68701R named *Bloody*, which was part of 'B' Squadron's 10 Troop. Commanded by Sergeant R.B. Lee, it was disabled when the right track was destroyed by shellfire on the tank's return to the beach. *Bloody* had towed the armoured car *Hunter* ashore.

Opposite bottom: The F2 in the square on the rear of this Churchill Mk.II identifies it as *Backer*, which was commanded by Lieutenant R.H. Wallace. Allocated to 'B' Squadron's 'F' Troop, it was the second tank to unload from its landing craft.

6-pounder gun, a Besa positioned to the left of it, and a Besa in the hull.[35] A number of the tanks were also fitted with Beach Track Laying devices or 'Bobbins'. The latter involved the fitting of a reel of ten-feet wide canvas cloth reinforced with steel poles – referred to as chespaling – on the front of the tank. When deployed, this unrolled onto the ground to form a 'path' along which the tank and any following vehicles could advance, hopefully not sinking into the soft ground of the beach or catching hard stones in any tracks.

According to the Calgary Regiment's War Diary the general tank plan was that all tanks would land in successive waves. 'C' Squadron would assist the Essex Scottish in establishing the bridgehead and taking care of the armed trawlers in the harbour. It would then cross to the high ground at the east side of the River D'Arques to dominate the approaches from the east. 'B' Squadron was to assist the Hamiltons in establishing the right flank of the bridgehead. They would then push inland and take the aerodrome at St. Aubin with the Camerons. 'A' Squadron, meanwhile, was to be held in reserve and would land later. Once the beachhead was secure, the headquarters of the German 302 Infantry Division at Arques-la-Bataille would be captured by the Camerons, aided by either 'A' or 'B' Squadron depending on the tactical situation.[36]

Flight 1 consisted of three LCTs which went ashore some ten minutes behind schedule, between approximately 05.25 hours and 05.30 hours. The infantry was thus deprived of the valuable covering fire which the tanks might have given in the first crucial minutes.

The first of these landing craft, with 'C' Squadron's headquarters embarked, touched down on the eastern end of Red beach. On board were the tanks *Chief*, *Company* and *Calgary*, as well as a scout car. After landing all its vehicles, this landing craft was sunk by shore batteries as it withdrew.

The first Churchill to disembark was *Chief*, the tank of Major Allen Glenn, the Officer Commanding 'C' Squadron. *Chief* was one of those fitted with a Bobbin which was laid successfully. Glenn advanced to the high ridge of stones on the other side of which a the trench about seven feet deep that had been created by workmen removing pebbles for the construction of the German fortifications. These obstacles ran the entire length of the beach to the Casino. From this position Glenn had a good view of the promenade and both flanks of the beach and he decided that the spot would be suitable for his command post.

Behind *Chief* came *Company*. As it landed it began to turn right to follow *Chief* when a shell hit the left front drive wheel, breaking a track pin, and immobilizing the tank just in front of the ridge on the beach. Though *Company* could not move, she could still fire and her 2-pounder and Besa machine-gun in the turret continued to operate throughout the battle. The position in which *Company* had come to rest meant that its hull-mounted mortar could not be used. It was hit several times by German mortar bombs and the tank filled with smoke but none of the crew were injured.

The last out was *Calgary*. Commanded by Lieutenant Brice Douglas, it was towing a scout car that, in turn, was loaded up with 50lb bags of plastic explosive. The scout car disengaged itself from

THE DIEPPE RAID

Calgary as Douglas drove along the seawall towards the Casino looking for a place to cross onto the promenade. The scout car had not gone far when it was hit by tracer fire and burst into flames killing both men inside.

As it moved down White beach, *Calgary* lost its left track. As with *Company*, *Calgary* spent the rest of the raid firing its weapons in support of the infantry on predetermined targets, particularly the Casino and the tobacco factory.

Above: The dead, dying and wounded still lie on the beach as German troops secure the battlefield. The tank on the left is Lieutenant Wallace's *Backer*. (National Museum of Denmark)

Right: Pictured here in a similar state and view to *Backer* is one of the Churchills from 'B' Squadron's 6 Troop. Nicknamed *Bob*, *Bert* and *Bill*, all three carried a number 6 in a square as an identification number. Judging by this tank's location, it is almost certainly *Bert* which was commanded by Squadron Sergeant-Major Gerry M. Menzies – the other two were stranded nearer the water's edge. *Bert* had managed to reach a position near the Casino (out of view to the left) when its port track was blown off.

TANK ATTACK

THE DIEPPE RAID

TANK ATTACK

The second landing craft, carrying 'C' Squadron's 13 Troop, came under from heavy fire from an assortment of coastal artillery, anti-aircraft guns, machine-guns and mortars. Nevertheless, it reached the shore near the jetty at the eastern end of the beach. As with the Headquarters troop, the first Churchill down the ramp, commanded by Troop Leader Lieutenant Thomas Cornett, was fitted with a Bobbin. *Cougar* also successfully laid its chespaling track as it crossed the beach and climbed over the seawall.

Next out was *Cheetah* which also crossed the beach and began climbing the wall. But as it reared up to mount the wall, its exposed underside was hit by a shell, though it eventually climbed the seawall and reached the promenade. Finding no infantry for them to support, *Cheetah*'s crew were unsure of what effective action they could take next. Also, more formidable obstacles than the wall were the heavy concrete roadblocks barring the streets leading out of the promenade into the town. These were reported to be eight feet high and four feet thick with a firing step on the rear. To breach these with explosives was the engineers' business; but some of the demolition parties had not landed, others had had equipment destroyed, and others had suffered casualties.

Finally, the third of 13 Troop's Churchills, *Cat*, got stuck halfway between the ramp of the landing craft and the beach. The captain of the landing craft reversed engines, pulling the ramp away to allow the tank to drop down onto the beach. At exactly the same moment a shell burst on the ramp and broke its cables which helped *Cat*, and the scout car *Hector*, to get clear. *Cat* also climbed the seawall, as did *Hector*, but the last that was seen of the scout car was it 'tearing like hell up Foch Boulevard' which ran along the seafront.

Cat joined *Cougar* on the promenade, the latter being struck by a shell from a 75mm coastal gun positioned on the far side of the canal below the eastern headland. *Cat* quickly responded with its 6-pounder, silencing the enemy gun. But the shell had smashed into *Cougar*'s turret ring which jammed. *Cougar* could then only aim its gun by turning the tank. It manoeuvred round to direct its fire at the tobacco factory only for its left track to break due to chert pebbles from the beach which were still lodged between the bogey wheel and the treads. *Cougar* could still pivot on one track, but this was also blown off by enemy gunfire. With little option, its crew abandoned their Churchill and returned to the beach to seek shelter.

Cat and *Cheetah*, on the other hand, being unable to force their way past the roadblocks into the town, cruised up and down the esplanade for hours, firing their machine-guns at the German positions in the sea-front buildings and trenches, and the 6-pounders at enemy strongpoints at the Casino and on the headlands.

Opposite top: A German soldier examines the Churchill tank *Cheetah*, which was from 'C' Squadron's 13 Troop. Despite being hit by a shell, which blew out all the fuses and necessitating emergency repairs, *Cheetah*, commanded by Corporal G.H. Wiggins, eventually made it over the seawall and up onto the promenade area. By the end of the attack *Cheetah* was the most easterly of the tanks, lying closest to the West Jetty.

Opposite bottom: Lying a short distance to the west of *Cheetah* was *Cat*, seen here with a German soldier peering in through the side hatch. Commanded by Sergeant J. Weaver, *Cat* came ashore as part of 'C' Squadron's 13 Troop. Having been forced to abandon their charges, the crew of *Cheetah* and two wounded men from *Cat* sheltered together beside the former tank, though they were continually fired upon by snipers positioned on the West Jetty. Note the damage to the buildings in the background. (Bundesarchiv, CC-BY-SA 3.0)

THE DIEPPE RAID

This spread: The stranded Churchill Mk.I of Major C.E. Page, CO of 'B' Squadron. Quickly out of its landing craft, *Burns* ploughed up the beach, at which point it was hit and the right track knocked off. It did not move from the spot where it was later photographed.

The two tanks became the target of German aircraft, which attacked the Churchills repeatedly but without success until one bomb eventually hit *Cat*'s engine and it had to be abandoned. For its part, *Cheetah* survived until it was making its way to the beach when a bomb hit the engine compartment and it too had to be left where it lay.

As the LCT carrying a bulldozer and 8 Troop of 'B' Squadron closed to around 100 yards from the shore, one of the Royal Navy ratings lowered the ramp about halfway to allow Troop Leader Captain Douglas Purdy in *Bull* to see the beach. Believing that the ramp was being lowered because they had reached the shore, Purdy ordered his driver to set off. The tank moved off onto the ramp, which collapsed. Water rushed into the landing craft and into *Bull* which was nose-down in the sea. Realising that the craft was being dragged under, the captain went into reverse and put the helm about from side to side to try and shake off the tank.

The landing craft eventually dislodged *Bull* which sank in approximately ten feet of water. The Churchills had been waterproofed to wade through water to a depth of just six feet. Purdy could not swim and, despite the efforts of Trooper Aide to save him, he drowned. Trooper William Stewart was also lost at sea, but the other two crewmen reached the shore.

Having rid itself of *Bull* the landing craft, now without its ramp, went forward again to land the rest of 8 Troop but a shell struck the wheelhouse, killing all inside. The vessel drifted to a halt in shallow water to the west of a tobacco factory. This enabled the remaining vehicles to bump down from the vessel onto the beach. Purdy's 8 Troop was fitted with flamethrowers and the first out, *Boar*, smashed off its fuel tank as it dropped onto the beach. *Boar* reached the promenade near the Casino.

Like the tanks of 'C' Squadron, *Boar* drove along the promenade being unable to penetrate the town until the crew were ordered to return to the beach.

The unfortunate story of 8 Troop continued when the third tank, *Beetle*, found itself unable to move forward as one of the wheel chocks had not been removed. The driver put the tank into reverse and in doing so drove over, and crushed to death, two wounded men. After landing heavily on the beach *Beetle* headed for the seawall opposite the Casino only for one of the tracks to break due to a build-up of chert stones. *Beetle* ground to a halt at the interface between Red and White beaches where it gave protection to some of the infantry and from where it fired upon German positions on the western headland.

'B' Squadron's 'F' Troop, carrying the Squadron Headquarters, landed on White beach to the east of the tobacco factory without incident, but all three tanks soon ran into trouble. The first Churchill out onto the beach was *Burns* commanded by Major Page. *Burns* crossed the beach as far as the trench by the seawall when it was hit, and the right track was blown off. With the tank facing downwards into the trench its guns were useless. Page ordered the tank to be abandoned.

Opposite top: The Daimler Scout car seen here in the foreground, *Helen* of 'B' Squadron's headquarters troop, was landed on White beach by TLC-4 (No.126) soon after the first wave had gone ashore. Note the bullet holes across the hull. In the landing craft with *Helen* were the Churchill tanks named *Burns*, *Blacker* and *Bolster*. Behind *Helen*, and a little to the right, is *Beetle* – its flamethrower can be seen on the front of the hull pointing up at the sky.

Opposite bottom: Like *Helen*, *Bolster*, a Mk.I, would also become stranded on the beach. Part of HQ Fighting Troop, 'B' Squadron, it was commanded by Sergeant T.R. Cunningham and was disabled when the right track was broken by chert build-up. *Bolster* had towed *Helen* ashore.

TANK ATTACK

Above: German personnel inspect an abandoned Daimler Scout car near the promenade at Dieppe. The number 9 in the diamond on the side of the hull suggests that this is *Hector*, which was landed as part of 'C' Squadron's 13 Troop. Crewed by Trooper Edward Anderson and Trooper Art Buckley, *Hector* was the only Scout car to cross over the seawall and penetrate parts of the town itself before returning to the beach, at which point it suffered the effects of a mortar bomb. (Bundesarchiv, Bild 101I-291-1207-11/Koll/CC-BY-SA 3.0)

Below: The Daimler Scout car *Hound*, which, indicated by the number 2 in the diamond, was towed ashore by Churchill tank *Confident* – both from 'C' Squadron's 15 Troop. In the melee ashore, not helped by the fact that the tank was struck by a shell (fortunately a dud), *Confident*'s crew completely forgot about the Scout car being dragged behind them. Whilst manoeuvring, the tank slammed into *Hound*, leaving it partially buried as seen here. (Bundesarchiv, Bild 101I-362-2211-02/Jörgensen/CC-BY-SA 3.0)

Similar fates as those above were suffered by the other Churchills. Disabled either by enemy fire or the chert, the tanks either failed to escape the beach or trundled aimlessly along the seafront.

Only two members of the tank crews who landed managed to get away and return to the UK – the remainder were either killed or taken prisoner. Nos. 11, 12, and 14 Troops of 'C' Squadron and the whole of 'A' Squadron remained afloat during the operation, laying offshore awaiting orders to go in. About 13.00 hours, the order was given to return to England.[37]

Among the losses that day was the Calgary's CO, Lieutenant-Colonel John Andrews. The incident was recorded in the regimental War Diary: 'The Landing Craft Tank (LCT) carrying regimental HQ went onto the beach in the 3rd wave, under cover of smoke … As it approached the shore with its door partly lowered, the chains supporting the door were blown away, and the door dropped under the LCT preventing it from getting any closer to the shore. The Colonel's tank at once drove off the ship, tearing a louvre extension, and sank into six feet of water and stalled. The crew abandoned the tank and the Colonel was seen to get into an "R" boat. Almost immediately this boat was set ablaze, and the Colonel was last seen swimming in the water.'[38] It is believed that he was killed by gunfire.

One German summed up the actions of the Calgary Regiment that morning: 'We counted 28 heavy tanks trying to enter the city, and behind them, the Tommies. Only 2 tanks managed to reach within 15 metres of the first houses at the beach. It was there that they broke down with mangled tracks. The others struggled to get across the rocky beach … Our heavy anti-tank guns and artillery took out the remaining tanks on the beach with direct fire. They were completely destroyed.'[39]

Below: Another abandoned Daimler Scout car on the beach at Dieppe. In this case it is *Hunter*, which was allocated to 'B' Squadron's 10 Troop. As well as its driver, Trooper Michael Zima, it was carrying Major Gordon Rolfe, Royal Canadian Corps of Signals, and two No.19 wireless sets. Rolfe managed to keep both sets operational throughout the attack. Note the knocked-out Jeep in the centre background. (Bundesarchiv, Bild 101I-362-2211-04/Jörgensen/CC-BY-SA 3.0)

THE DIEPPE RAID

Thi spread: Though they are not all in perfect focus, the selection of images seen on these two pages, taken privately by a German soldier soon after the fighting on 19 August, provides further views of

Bert. Commanded by Squadron Sergeant-Major Gerry M. Menzies, this Churchill was knocked-out near the Casino. *Bert* can also be seen on page 83. Menzies, meanwhile, also appears on page 150.

THE DIEPPE RAID

Left: Bodies of the fallen still lie among abandoned Churchill tanks. The latter are believed to be, right to left, *Boar*, *Buttercup* and *Bluebell*.

Below: This tank, Mk.I T31878R named *Company*, was part of HQ Fighting Troop, 'C' Squadron. It was transported aboard TLC 1. Commanded by Captain George Valentine, it was disabled when the left front idler wheel was hit by shell fire. The Calgary Regiment's Medical Officer, Dr. Laurence Guy Alexander, would later write that 'when last heard from over the radio Valentine was displaying amazing courage and fighting a gallant fight'.

THE DIEPPE RAID

Main image: The imposing Château de Dieppe looks down on the battlefield in the aftermath of *Jubilee*. The abandoned Churchill that can be seen just left of centre is that named *Beetle*. This was a flamethrower tank of 8 Troop, 'B' Squadron, serial number T68875, which was commanded by Lieutenant Gordon Drysdale. Just visible on the rear of hull, in fact with the name *Beetle* on it, is the armoured fuel tank that formed part of the flamethrower equipment. Just beyond *Beetle* is the Daimler Scout car *Helen*. In the right foreground is Captain Austin Stanton's Mk.II *Ringer*. Stanton was the Calgary's Adjutant. No sooner has his tank exited the landing craft then it became bogged down in the loose shale.

TANK ATTACK

THE DIEPPE RAID

TANK ATTACK

Main image: A German soldier picks his way through the abandoned equipment and the bodies of some of the fallen on the main beach at Dieppe. On the left is *Backer*, while, on the right, closer to the beached TLC 3, is Lieutenant E. Bennet's Mk.III, *Bellicose* of 'B' Squadron's 10 Troop.

THE DIEPPE RAID

Above: German servicemen pose for the camera while sat on Lieutenant Bennet's *Bellicose*. (Courtesy of S. Pallad)

Below: A number of abandoned Churchill tanks litter the shoreline in this view taken looking west down the beach at Dieppe. In the foreground, on the right, is Lieutenant Brice Douglas' Mk.III named *Calgary*. Dominating the scene, once again, is the still burning LCT-5 (No.121).

Chapter 10

THE AERIAL BATTLE AT DIEPPE

Though much of the narrative around Operation *Jubilee* centres on the landing forces and the Royal Navy's efforts to get them ashore, and rightly so, the events of 19 August 1942 also saw the Allied air forces, and in particular the RAF, undertake an intensity of sorties that had not really been seen since the dark days of the summer of 1940. That this effort is often overlooked is partly the result of the fact that much of the aerial activity, as had been the case at Dunkirk just over two years before, took place away from the beaches and, therefore, out of sight of those battling away on the ground.

Below: The aerial aspect of Operation *Jubilee* was directed by Air Vice-Marshal Trafford Leigh-Mallory from the Headquarters of 11 Group, Fighter Command at Uxbridge. Whilst Leigh-Mallory, Air Officer Commanding 11 Group, was designated the Air Force Commander, the immediate operations of the Allied fighters were directed by the fighter controller in HMS *Calpe*. This picture of Leigh-Mallory was taken at Uxbridge on 27 March 1942.

Above: Douglas Boston Mk.IIIs, believed to be of 88 Squadron, lined up at RAF Attlebridge, Norfolk, in preparation for their involvement in the Dieppe Raid, August 1942.

Right: Aircrew of either 88 Squadron or 107 Squadron being briefed at RAF Ford, Sussex, before taking off to support the attack on Dieppe. Their targets were German gun batteries. Visible in the background is a Douglas Havoc or Boston night intruder of 605 (County of Warwick) Squadron.

The air force resources assigned to *Jubilee* were impressive. The aerial armada included fifty-six squadrons of day fighters (of which fifty were to provide direct cover, the remaining six being tasked with close support), two squadrons of Hurricanes acting in the ground-attack role, two squadrons of day bombers, four squadrons of Army Co-operation aircraft, and three squadrons detailed as the 'Smoke forces'. This was a total of sixty-seven squadrons.[40]

THE AERIAL BATTLE AT DIEPPE

103

THE AERIAL BATTLE AT DIEPPE

Main image: A group of pilots from 401 Squadron RCAF pictured between sorties on 19 August 1942. Among the five men are Flight Sergeant Ed Gimbel, Flight Lieutenant Jim Whitham, Flight Sergeant Bob Reesor, and Pilot Officer 'Scotty' Murray.

In addition, Coastal Command provided search patrols during the passage of the expedition throughout the hours of darkness hours. Douglas Bostons also carried out bombing attacks on the east headland battery at 05.10 hours, after which a smoke screen was laid over both headlands. The two batteries behind the town were also targeted by Bostons, but owing to the haze and the bad light these attacks on the batteries were considered in the words of Chief of Combined Operations 'quite ineffective'.

Alongside these sorties, RAF Intruders engaged batteries, cannon-fighters supported the landing of the troops on Red and White beaches, and further smoke screens were also laid as requested by the Naval and Military force commanders. Subsequent bombing attacks were made on the east headland when it was seen that the landings on Blue beach were held up. Unfortunately, the bombs, like the destroyers' shells, had little effect on the more permanent German defences. Nor can it be said that the bombing was very intensive, for the total of bombs dropped amounted only to some 220 bombs of 500lbs, and about ninety of 250lbs – a total of sixty tons.

Flying a Hawker Hurricane of 174 Squadron, Flight Sergeant John William Brooks was one of the pilots tasked with the ground-attack role. 'It was quite easy to make out the coast and the town of Dieppe …', he later recalled, adding that the 'flak and fireworks were on par to 5th November'.

Losing altitude and confronted by intense anti-aircraft fire, Brooks searched out his target. 'Then I saw it. Three or four big splodges of German concrete surrounded by trees. I called up my section and told them "Target ahead" … I went down as low as I dared to release my bombs – I couldn't really miss. I could make out the heavy guns in their white concrete bases along with some smaller gun sites and huts. It was these smaller sites which had the guns which were firing at me, so I fired back as I dived down. This is a general tactic to make the people on the ground keep their heads down. Eight machine guns all going at once are quite noisy.

'I pulled out at a couple of hundred feet and saw the trees loom out of the darkness in front of me. My bombs had a 6-second delay whilst the boys behind me had 2-second fuses. This was to prevent those behind me from being blown up by my bombs. Nevertheless, it still needed a quick and coordinated run over the target even with these precautions. After what seemed a very long time, I saw the whole site go up in a series of quick flashes and then felt the crump which bounced my Hurricane about.'[41]

At the beginning of Operation *Jubilee* there was practically no Luftwaffe opposition, but as time passed Göring's squadrons began to swing into action. As the German fighters became airborne, the early appearances were made by groups of between twenty and thirty fighters. Gradually the strength of these attacks increased to between fifty and 100 aircraft.

One witness on the ground remembered the sight presented by some of the first Luftwaffe aircraft: 'As we talked, the air almost at cliff-top height over our heads was suddenly full of fighters snarling, screaming and twisting in a dogfight … I could see the heads of the Germans in their Focke-Wulf 190s, and of the R.A.F. pilots in their Spitfires.'[42]

Numerous German fighter bombers were deployed, and a number of abortive attacks were carried out on the Allied ships. But it was not until about 10.00 hours that the first of the Luftwaffe's heavier bombers appeared, these being escorted by fighters. Confronted by masses of RAF fighters, the enemy bombers sustained severe losses. They made no attempt to attack the troops ashore and confined their attentions to the ships, but except for the sinking of HMS *Berkeley*, had practically no success.

The air battle reached its greatest intensity during the main withdrawal from the beaches. During this phase of the raid, Bostons again bombed targets on the two headlands, and a heavy smoke

THE AERIAL BATTLE AT DIEPPE

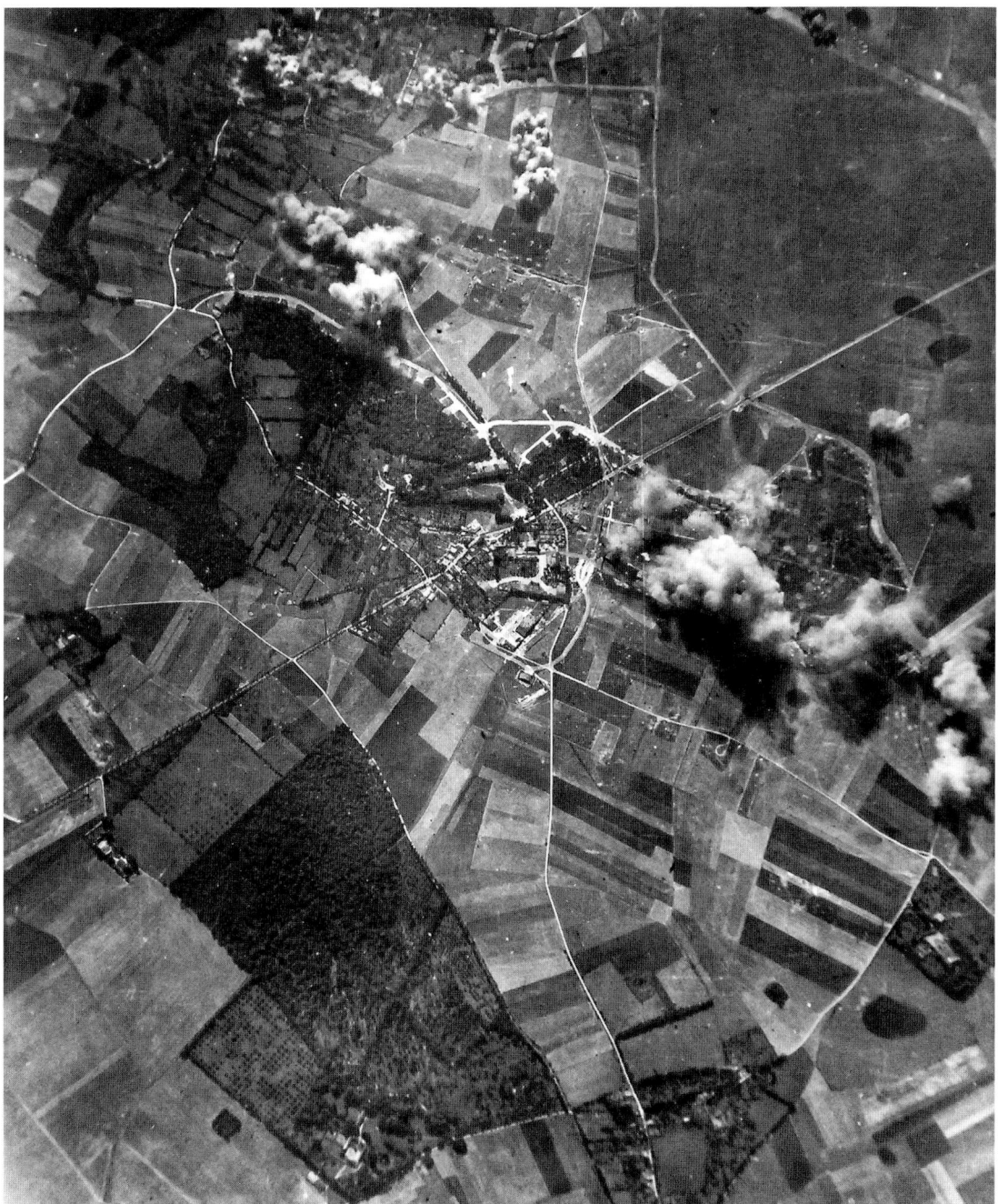

Above: At 10.30 hours an attack was made by a force of twenty-four USAAF B-17 Flying Fortresses, escorted by RAF Spitfires, on the Luftwaffe fighter airfield at Abbeville-Drucat. This bombing rendered the airfield unserviceable for two hours and probably severely hampered the enemy fighters at the crucial moment of the withdrawal. Here bombs from the Flying Fortresses fall on the aerodrome. (NARA)

THE DIEPPE RAID

THE AERIAL BATTLE AT DIEPPE

Left: Another image taken during the USAAF attack on Abbeville-Drucat on 19 August 1942. Of the twenty-four bombers involved, twenty-two actually bombed the target. The bombing was reported to be very accurate. (NARA)

Below: The USAAF crew of one of the Boeing B-17 Flying Fortresses which participated in air operations supporting the Dieppe Raid 'leave their plane somewhere in Britain'. *Dixie Demo* was assigned to the 414th Bomb Squadron, 97th Bomb Group at the time. This aircraft had participated in the USAAF's first operational mission from the UK just two days earlier. (NARA)

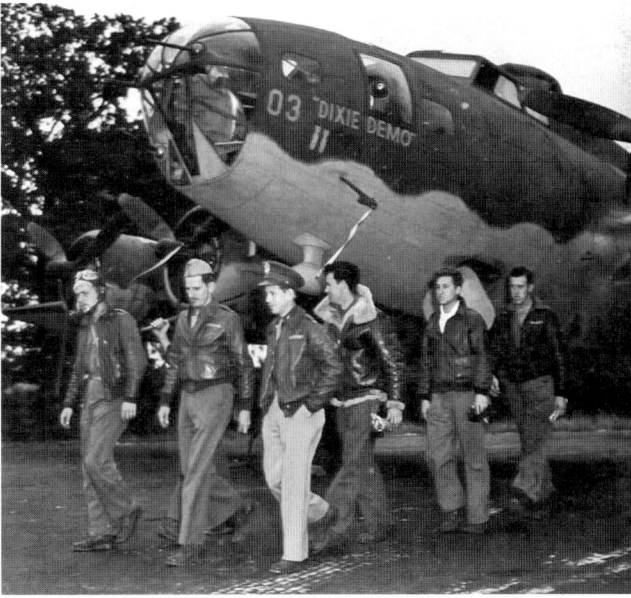

curtain was laid from the air. From 12.00 hours, heavy battles between formations of fighters went on over the ships and beaches. During the voyage home, fighter cover was maintained over the Allied armada and all attempts by enemy aircraft to attack the ships were foiled.

In the air the RAF lost eight bombers and smoke layers, ten Army Co-operation and reconnaissance aircraft, and eighty-eight

Above: A USAAF airman, 2nd Lieutenant Samuel S. Junkin Jr., is pictured at a Canadian Army hospital in Britain after Operation *Jubilee*. He had just been presented with two United States awards – the Distinguished Flying Cross and the Purple Heart. He was decorated by Brigadier General F.O.D. Hunter, Commanding General, Fighter Command, US Eighth Air Force, while in the hospital recovering from wounds received during a mission in support of the Dieppe Raid. Left to right are Brigadier General H.A. Craig, Brigadier General L.I. Truscott, Jr., Captain A.H. Willetts RAF, Brigadier General F.O.D. Hunter, and Second Lieutenant Junkin. (NARA)

Right: One of the many aircrew who saw action during Operation *Jubilee* – Wing Commander Daniel Le Roy Du Vivier. Du Vivier was the first non-Commonwealth national to attain the rank of Wing Commander in the RAF. Regarding Dieppe, at the time it was noted that, 'He undertook 4 attacks on heavily defended enemy positions coming back time after time with a damaged aircraft. His heroism is once more rewarded by his RAF superiors who awarded him a "Bar" on the ribbon of his DFC.' In his book *The Greatest Air Battle*, the late Norman Franks reports that Du Vivier, flying the 43 Squadron Hurricane Mk.II BN230, coded 'FT-A', was 'the first fighter pilot over Dieppe that day'. Norman adds that 'he led his pilots in twice, flying in line abreast and turning to port after each attack'.

THE AERIAL BATTLE AT DIEPPE

THE DIEPPE RAID

THE AERIAL BATTLE AT DIEPPE

Above: One of the early RAF losses of Operation *Jubilee* was 43 Squadron's Pilot Officer A.E. Snell, who was shot down at the controls of Hurricane Mk.II BP703, coded 'FT-O'. Flying in the same early morning attack as Du Vivier – strikes made just as it was beginning to get light – Snell reported that he had been hit and was baling out. Rescued by a passing landing craft, Snell spent the rest of the day manning a machine-gun. (Courtesy of Chris Goss)

Opposite: An RAF pilot or airman being rescued from the waters of the English Channel during Operation *Jubilee*. In total, it is stated that the total number of Allied sorties flown on 19 August 1942 was in the order of 3,000.

Above: His head bandaged, Flight Sergeant Robert Mehew 'Zip' Zobell of 401 Squadron RCAF, is pictured by his damaged Spitfire on his return from a sortie over Dieppe on 19 August. The original caption states that 'his only complaint was that the medical officer would not allow him to fly during the rest of the day'.

fighters. The casualties in terms of aircrew were 113 killed and missing, with a further forty wounded.

One of the many RAF aircraft lost that day was the 226 Squadron Boston, Al680 and coded MQ-L, flown by Pilot Officer Kenneth Warwood. It was their second sortie of the day that ended in disaster: '[It was] an aircraft fitted with smoke installation things to lay smokescreens. They looked like Calor gas cylinders. Four of us went back to Dieppe in the afternoon. We let go the smoke which came out of the bomb bays and then turned in towards land.

'We got hit in the port engine and it was just hanging off because of a direct hit from a shore battery. We then lost the canopy, and then the whole tail was shot off. We flopped into the water as were only at about ten feet.

'I had thrown my helmet off, and the next thing, I woke up. I had been thrown through the nose, which luckily had no Perspex due to the flak hit. I still had my "K" type dinghy and seat and was thrown about 40 yards into the water.'[43]

Of the Allied losses, one Canadian official historian noted that, 'The RAF had to fight the enemy in his own air, close to his own fields, and the initial advantage of surprise was lost long before the battle was over. The gallant and successful fight waged in support of the operation against the highly-organized German air defence cost the Allied squadrons a total of 106 aircraft … the RAF's heaviest loss in the air in a single day since the war began, and indeed the heaviest of the whole war.'

THE AERIAL BATTLE AT DIEPPE

Above: The Official History of the Dieppe Raid states that 'it is estimated that the enemy made 125 sorties with bombers and 600 with fighters'. This picture shows crews from KG 6 being briefed for attacks on 19 August 1942. (Courtesy of Chris Goss)

One of the many Luftwaffe pilots that flew over Dieppe on 19 August was Leutnant Leopold Wenger of 10./JG 2. Having taken-off at 10.33 hours, he would later recall his impressions of the area around the town: 'When we arrived over Dieppe, the fighting zone was shrouded in mist, dust and dense smoke. The fleet was completely hidden. Everywhere there were muzzle flashes and ashore you could see lots of fires from shot down aircraft and burnt out tanks. In the sea, many aircrew were floating in their rubber dinghies. At exactly midday, we began a low-level attack. At the same moment, a German bomber dived past us into the sea. We advanced in the mist and got to the cause of the smoke screen.

'All our guns were fired and bombs released at the same time. A bomb went off under the stern of a destroyer, but then I was shot at by all kinds of flak and because of the fireworks, I couldn't watch any more. The three other 190s flying with me damaged a few more ships, and one shot down a Spitfire. Still flying at low level, we fired into the packed landing craft. The effect was devastating.'[44]

It is estimated that the Luftwaffe made 125 sorties with bombers and 600 with fighters. As one Official History noted, 'At the time it was thought that the enemy's air losses were considerably greater than ours and that over a quarter of the German Air Force in Western Europe had been put out of action. German records show, however, that in fact we only destroyed 23 fighters and 25 bombers, while 8 fighters and 16 bombers were damaged.'

THE DIEPPE RAID

The same account went on to state the following: 'These bare figures, however, do not tell the whole story. According to reliable German documents, there were in the Luftflotte 3 area (France, Belgium and Holland) 299 fighters and 175 bombers, but of these only 206 fighters and 107 bombers were fully serviceable at the time. Thus about 15% of the serviceable fighters and over 38% per cent of the serviceable bombers were either destroyed or substantially damaged … Coming just after substantial losses suffered in the raids on Birmingham at the end of July, the casualties at Dieppe were a heavy blow, particularly as nearly all of the crews were lost, including two Squadron Commanders.'[45]

As the late Norman Franks noted in his book *The Greatest Air Battle*, 'By the end of that August day in 1942, the Royal Air Force and the German Luftwaffe had fought what must be regarded as the greatest air of the war if only in terms of aeroplanes lost in combat on both sides in the space of just sixteen hours'. In conclusion, he stated that 'Despite the tragic losses suffered by the Canadian troops on the ground, the RAF claimed a great victory that day'.[46]

Above: Squadron Leader Lloyd Chadburn pictured in front of his Spitfire. For his part in Operation *Jubilee* with 416 Squadron RCAF, Chadburn was awarded the Distinguished Flying Cross. Chadburn claimed his first victories covering the Dieppe Raid.

Opposite: The damage to the fuel tank of a 3 Squadron Hawker Hurricane, more specially BE371, sustained in combat over Dieppe on 19 August 1942. (Courtesy of Chris Goss)

THE DIEPPE RAID

Left: Once again the result of a *Jubilee*-related combat, daylight can be seen through the wing of Spitfire EP559 of 312 Squadron. (Courtesy of Chris Goss)

Right: In his book *The Greatest Air Battle*, the late Norman Franks described 25-year-old Oberfeldwebel Josef 'Sepp' Würmheller of 9/JG 2, seen here, as the 'most outstanding Luftwaffe fighter pilot of the day'. Norman went on to recount the following, all of which reveals the extent of the air activity that day: 'On the morning of 19 August he was in fact suffering from a broken foot and had his lower leg encased in plaster bandage. However, when the alarm came and the huge Allied effort was revealed, Würmheller was helped into his Focke Wulf and took off. Not long after take-off his machine developed engine trouble and he had to force-land in a field. He hobbled to a German command post from where he was returned to his airfield by car. He had banged his head in the landing but in spite of a raging headache, climbed into another 190 and headed for the battle. Over Dieppe he claimed one Blenheim and two Spitfires, before returning home to refuel and rearm. On his second sortie he claimed three Spitfires and then later on his fourth flight over the ships shot down another Spitfire … During his final sortie his headache had got so bad that he flew with a veil before his vision. At the end of the day a doctor discovered that his head injury had in fact caused a concussion.' (Courtesy of Chris Goss)

Below: As the bitter battle for survival continued to rage on the beaches at Dieppe, this still from a German newsreel shows fighters racing low over the seafront. (Critical Past)

THE DIEPPE RAID

Left: During the withdrawal RAF Bostons made bombing attacks on the two headlands, and a heavy smoke curtain was laid from the air. Here, a Douglas Boston Mk.III of 88 Squadron, flying from Ford in Sussex, heads inland over France after the bombing the German gun batteries defending Dieppe. The original caption, dated 20 August 1942, states: 'The fiercest air battles since the Battle of Britain were fought by the RAF and the newest RAF Command, Army Co-operation, during the biggest-ever Combined Operations raid on Dieppe on August 19th. A total of 88 enemy machines was destroyed for certain, with 100 more probables. Canadian and United Kingdom Special Service Troops carried out the raid, with a detachment of a US Ranger Battalion and a small contingent of Fighting French. The force was carried and escorted by the Royal Navy. Picture shows a Boston aircraft over France and approaching the target.'

Top right: Another of the Luftwaffe pilots to make a claim during *Jubilee* was Oberleutnant Siegfried 'Wumm' Schnell, the Staffelkapitän of 9 Staffel of II Gruppe, JG 2. He would claim the destruction of five Spitfires in the skies over Dieppe, bringing his personal tally to seventy. (Courtesy of Chris Goss)

Bottom right: Oberfeldwebel Kurt Goltzsch of 4./JG 2 also claimed success during the dogfights on 19 August 1942. Having achieved his first victory in the Battle of Britain while serving with 8./JG 2, Goltzsch was seriously wounded when he was shot down in aerial combat on 4 September 1943. The Staffelkapitän of 5./JG 2 at the time, he broke his back and was left paralysed when his Messerschmitt Bf 109 crash-landed. He succumbed to his wounds on 26 September 1944. (Courtesy of Chris Goss)

THE DIEPPE RAID

Main image: The Luftwaffe sorties over the Dieppe area led to the largest Royal Navy loss of the operation. Whilst it was bombarding houses at the back of White beach, the Hunt-class destroyer HMS *Berkeley*, pennant number L17, received the signal to withdraw. On arriving at the rendezvous point, *Berkeley*'s Captain, Lieutenant James Yorke, intended to turn round astern of the main body in order to make smoke and provide some cover for the evacuation. This picture of *Berkeley* was taken by a photographer from the Photographic Section of the School of Naval Co-operation, which was based at RAF Ford, in October 1940. At the time, *Berkeley* was in the Solent, as evidenced by the presence of one of the Solent Forts and, on the shore, the Portsmouth Naval Memorial.

Right: While HMS *Berkeley* was preparing to make smoke, at 13.18 hours she was attacked by three Dorniers which were at once engaged by Allied fighters. Undeterred, Luftwaffe aircraft continued the assault on the destroyer. One of those who witnessed these attacks was Group Captain Harry 'Broadie' Broadhurst DSO, DFC, AFC, who flew four sorties that day; he had taken off from RAF Hornchurch at 12.30 hours on the third of these. 'The withdrawal was almost complete,' he later recalled, 'and with the exception of a few ships two or three miles off Dieppe, which included the destroyer *Berkeley*, the convoy was in full progress back towards the English coast … I noticed that the rear of the convoy, i.e. that part of it nearest to the French coast, was being subjected to the most severe attacks and latterly the majority being directed against the destroyer *Berkeley* … Towards the end of my patrol I saw two Focke-Wulfs dive towards the *Berkeley*. I dived after them but could not intercept until after they had dropped their bombs, one of which appeared to score a direct hit on the stern of the *Berkeley*.' This picture shows HMS *Berkeley* in the moments after being hit. (Courtesy of Chris Goss)

THE AERIAL BATTLE AT DIEPPE

THE DIEPPE RAID

Below: One Fw 190 pilot who hit HMS *Berkeley* was Leutnant Leopold Wenger of 10./JG 2, who is standing second from the left in this photograph. Of his part in the attack, Wenger later recalled the following to the author and historian Chris Goss: 'The English [*sic*] were withdrawing everywhere, but the smoke screen did not help them much. I attacked a second destroyer and achieved a direct hit amidships with an SC500 bomb. During the attack, I was under heavy anti-aircraft fire from the destroyer but when the bomb went off, the guns stopped shooting. An explosion followed – simply disastrous. The whole ship was enveloped in a black cloud but then I was chased and attacked by many Spitfires and unfortunately could not watch the complete sinking.' (Courtesy of Chris Goss)

Above: An official report into *Jubilee* notes that, 'two bombs hit the ship (HMS *Berkeley*) on the starboard side just forward of the bridge. The ship's back was broken, the main bulkhead at the after end of the forward mess-deck was shattered, and the forepart of the ship was flooded.' Rescuers immediately made their way to assist HMS *Berkeley*. The gunboat SGB.8, for example, went alongside and took off the greater part of the destroyer's company – as shown in this image. Lieutenant Yorke still thought that there was a chance of saving his ship and decided to remain on board with a towing party. As, however, all communications on board had broken down and the ship appeared to be sinking, he reluctantly gave the order to abandon ship. This was carried out at 13.21 hours, at which point SGB.8 cast off. (Courtesy of Chris Goss)

THE DIEPPE RAID

Main image: At least thirteen members of HMS *Berkeley*'s crew were killed in the attack (though accounts vary, with some sources stating fifteen), along with an unknown number of army personnel. With all the survivors and bodies taken off, HMS *Albrighton* was ordered to sink the stricken destroyer. This was done through the firing of a pair of torpedoes. The second of these hit *Berkeley*'s forward magazine. At 13.38 hours, just twenty minutes after the German attack, HMS *Berkeley* slipped beneath the waves. This is the moment that *Albrighton*'s torpedoes hit home. (Courtesy of Chris Goss)

THE AERIAL BATTLE AT DIEPPE

THE DIEPPE RAID

Left: In his post-action report, Lieutenant Yorke specifically mentioned the gallantry of Colonel Lorin B. Hillsinger USAAF. Hillsinger was acting as an air observer onboard the destroyer. One account states that during the bombing, 'a steel chest sliding across the deck sheared his leg just below the knee. With an improvised tourniquet around his severed leg, he crawled to the rail and plunged fifteen feet to Steam Gun Boat #8 waiting below. He continued as aircraft lookout while lying on its deck severely wounded. In England, some seventeen hours later, his severed leg got its first hospital attention.' For his actions at Dieppe, Hillsinger was awarded the US Distinguished Service Cross 'for extraordinary heroism in connection with military operations against an armed enemy in aerial combat while serving as Air Officer, attached to the HMS *Berkeley*, in action against enemy forces on 19 August 1942, during the Allied Raid on the French port of Dieppe'. This picture shows the moment that Colonel Hillsinger had returned to the air – he is climbing down from Hawker Hurricane V6844 at RAF Hendon after a flight on 4 May 1943. Hillsinger was the first USAAF officer permitted to return to operational flying after losing a limb. (NARA)

Below: Having returned to base, Pilot Officer H.L. Pedersen shows the damage caused to his Spitfire, AR272 coded 'SK-L', after being engaged by a German rear gunner in one of the Dorniers that he and his fellow 165 Squadron pilots encountered during the withdrawal phase. (Courtesy of Chris Goss)

THE DIEPPE RAID

Left: This pilot from I./JG 2 is pictured wounded after baling out during the aerial fighting over Dieppe. The Official History of the Dieppe Raid notes the following in respect of the Luftwaffe's losses that day: 'At the time it was thought that the enemy's air losses were considerably greater than ours and that over a quarter of the German Air Force in Western Europe had been put out of action. German records show, however, that in fact we only destroyed 23 fighters and 25 bombers, while 8 fighters and 16 bombers were damaged. These bare figures, however, do not tell the whole story. According to reliable German documents, there were in the Luftflotte 3 area (France, Belgium and Holland) 299 fighters and 175 bombers, but of these only 206 fighters and 107 bombers were fully serviceable at the time. Thus about 15% of the serviceable fighters and over 38% per cent of the serviceable bombers were either destroyed or substantially damaged.' (Courtesy of Chris Goss)

Chapter 11

THE WITHDRAWAL

As the battle ashore, and, as we have seen, in the air, raged on, the reports reaching HMS *Calpe* soon began to present a bleak picture, and the retreat of the craft carrying the Royal Marines and the return of those carrying the tanks which could not be embarked confirmed that the raid had completely failed.

Below: His head bandaged, a wounded Canadian soldier is helped by his colleagues during the withdrawal. It was at 11.00 hours that the landing craft began to go in to recover the troops ashore, covered by naval fire and RAF fighters. Indeed, the fighter force over Dieppe had by then been increased from three squadrons to six, and sometimes was as high as nine. During this phase of the operation, all of the LCA were sent into the same beaches as those on which they had originally landed to take off as many troops as possible as best they could and ferry them to the LCTs awaiting them about a mile from the shore.

THE DIEPPE RAID

THE WITHDRAWAL

A highly structured withdrawal plan had been put in place, with each designated unit given a time to commence its withdrawal from the start of the instruction 'Vanquish' being issued by the Force Commander. It was emphasised that the timing should be strictly adhered to as the RAF would help cover the evacuation.

For this, an imaginary 'bomb line' had been drawn inside which the troops could safely move back to the waiting craft while beyond which the RAF aircraft could unleash their bombs and rockets knowing there was no risk of 'friendly fire' incidents. The other key factor was that the raid was a one-tide operation, which meant a very narrow time frame for the re-embarkation of all the troops.

The original intention, had the raid gone according to plan, was to take most of the troops off the beaches in LCTs. However, Hughes-Hallett decided that such was the volume of enemy fire, he could not risk sending in any vessels other than the smaller LCAs and LCMs. Such a decision meant abandoning any tanks that might still be serviceable. All possible support was to be given by destroyers and the large LCFs.

Believing that Green Beach was safely held by the Saskatchewans and did not need the covering fire required on Red and White beaches, *Calpe* steered for the western end of the beach. As she closed with the shore, *Calpe* came under heavy small arms and machine-gun fire and the destroyer had to pull back. But, at around 11.30 hours, *Calpe* embarked two landing craft loads of troops, mostly wounded, from whom it was learned that there were still men waiting to come off at Green beach.

In fact, four landing craft had battled through to reach Green beach, though one of these was so badly damaged by gunfire it was unable to take to the water again. Though no radio signals were received by the Boat Pool waiting offshore, the senior Beach Master on Green beach, Lieutenant-Commander Redvers Prior, drew the attention of one of the vessels offshore by standing on top of a pillbox and using semaphore flag signals. Predictably, as well as attracting the attention of the landing craft he also drew fire from German machine-gunners and his brave action soon saw him wounded.

It was an LCA that had seen Prior's signal and it manoeuvred into Green beach, only to be driven back by enemy fire. Undaunted, Prior exposed himself a second and finally a third time until, at last, four landing craft arrived. Prior was wounded a total of four times.

With the tide now out, the men had to cross 200 yards of open beach to reach the landing craft. The wounded were embarked first, then Colonel Merritt ordered the second batch to go forward. 'Don't run, men,' he shouted. 'Slope arms and march to the beach!' This, wisely, stopped the men from rushing and panicking.

Among those who survived was Jack Nissenthall. He had moved down towards the beach with the remainder of the Canadian troops. It had become very clear that the Saskatchewans could not hold out much longer against the increasing numbers of enemy soldiers, and Nissenthall, the threat of execution hanging over him, was becoming understandably desperate to escape.

He watched a group of men run for Pourville beach. The Germans opened fire 'and the men who were hurrying to escape by running to the water to swim out to sea began falling like rag dolls'. The survivors scurried back to the protection of the seawall. Some, though, did get away and he saw another wave of men run from the seawall to throw themselves into the water to try and reach

Left: Still wearing his floatation aid, one wounded soldier is helped ashore from the ship that had transported him back to England. (National Museum of Denmark)

THE DIEPPE RAID

Right: Canadian troops clamber up onto the deck of a destroyer from their landing craft during the withdrawal. Of the 4,963 Canadians who embarked for the operation, 2,211 returned to England. Of these, however, it seems likely that nearly 1,000 had never landed. Analysis suggests that only between 350 and 400 men were evacuated from the main beaches in front of the town.

the landing craft hovering out at sea. 'That's when I decided that for myself it was now or never,' recalled Nissenthall.

With his little party and another ten or so, Nissenthall dashed for the sea. Only four made it through the murderous enemy fire to reach the waterline: 'We ran into the ebbtide, discarding helmets and equipment as we went, over the slippery, shining pebbles that hadn't yet dried in the sun, and splashed through the incoming waves, knee-deep, waist deep, chest-deep in the rising water, and plunged at last into the sea ... Bullets were splashing all around us ... I could see in the distance a landing-craft appearing from and disappearing back into, the billowing clouds of smoke drifting across the water.'[47] That landing craft plucked Nissenthall out of the water; he was one of only 353 who returned to the UK from Green beach out of 523 who had disembarked just a few hours earlier. That this number escaped was in large measure due to Colonel Merritt's self-sacrifice, holding the Germans at bay until the very last moment.

The withdrawal from Orange beach was as successful as No.4 Commandos' operation had been throughout. The medical officer, Captain Walker, and three of his medics were called forward from the beachhead with stretchers to take the wounded down to the shoreline. Doors from adjacent houses were ripped off their hinges to carry Pat Porteous and a couple of other badly wounded back to the beach.

Lovat ordered that the bodies of those who

THE WITHDRAWAL

THE DIEPPE RAID

THE WITHDRAWAL

had been killed be brought together in one spot and a Union Flag draped over them. The German dead were left where they had fallen.

The enemy had not been entirely subdued and throughout the withdrawal the Commandos were sniped at from the flanks of the road to the beach but there were no further casualties and a pre-arranged smoke screen from smoke generators shrouded the final movements onto the landing craft which began at around 07.30 hours. Forty-five minutes later the re-embarkation was complete and No.4 Commando was on its way home.

At about 11.30 hours HMS *Brocklesby* was ordered to close the Red and White beaches and give supporting fire. She advanced to within 500 yards of the beaches, firing at gun positions on the cliffs and at houses on the front, but her action did not appear to have had much effect on the enemy guns, which were firing on the main beaches. The destroyer itself came under very heavy fire and was repeatedly hit by shells and even by small-arms fire.

At 12.15 hours, according to *Brocklesby*'s report, the enemy was still firing from the Casino and large houses to the east of the building. Three LCT were high and dry and the troops were sheltering behind these, whilst others lying on the beach were still firing. The number of troops was estimated at between 100 and 150, with one man signalling for boats to be sent to rescue these few survivors.

At 12.33 house, the destroyer HMS *Fernie* attempted to give Red beach extra smoke cover but was hit and her gunfire director put out of action. Meanwhile, Commander Hubert McClintock, the Boat Pool officer, unable to find HMS *Calpe*, had made a signal at 12.20 hours saying that no further evacuation was possible. Roberts, though, asked for further efforts to be made to bring off troops and more than 400 men were evacuated from Red and White beaches under conditions of the greatest difficulty, the crews of the landing craft showing complete contempt for danger.

The evacuation from Dieppe beach was remarkable for the actions of one man, Honorary Captain John Weir Foote, Canadian Chaplain Services, who was Regimental Chaplain with the Royal Hamilton Light Infantry. His citation for the Victoria Cross details just some of his actions that day: 'During the action, as the tide went out, the Regimental Aid Post was moved to the shelter of a stranded landing craft. Honorary Captain Foote continued tirelessly and courageously to carry wounded men from the exposed beach to the cover of the landing craft. He also removed wounded from inside the landing craft when ammunition had been set on fire by enemy shells. When landing craft appeared he carried wounded from the Regimental Aid Post to the landing craft through very heavy fire.

'On several occasions this officer had the opportunity to embark but returned to the beach as his chief concern was the care and evacuation of the wounded. He refused a final opportunity to leave the shore, choosing to suffer the fate of the men he had ministered to for over three years.'[48]

At 12.40 hours Hughes-Hallett on HMS *Calpe* moved in close to the beaches for a final personal inspection. At just under a mile from the shore she came under heavy fire and, as no troops could be seen on the beach, *Calpe* retired behind the smoke screen.

It appeared impossible to bring off any more troops, but before finally abandoning the attempt Hughes-Hallett directed *Calpe* to close with *Locust*, which was bombarding the eastern cliff, intending to ask its captain, Commander Ryder, if he felt he could take his shallow-draught vessel in once more. At this time, however, Roberts received a signal saying that the remainder of the troops ashore were surrendering. Such was the inauspicious end to Mountbatten's super-raid.

Right: Men from No.3 Commando pictured on their arrival at Newhaven after the Dieppe Raid. As can be seen, they went into action wearing their steel helmets. (National Museum of the US Navy)

THE DIEPPE RAID

THE WITHDRAWAL

Left: The Polish Navy's destroyer ORP *Ślązak* arrives back at Portsmouth, from Dieppe, on 19 August 1942. *Ślązak* was one of eight Hunt-class destroyers assigned to *Jubilee*. During the withdrawal she was responsible for rescuing some eighty-men from the Royal Regiment of Canada.

Above: A wounded Captain J.C.H. 'Jock' Anderson of the Royal Regiment of Canada, cup of tea in hand, recounts his experiences to Brigadier Tees after disembarking at Portsmouth, 19 August 1942.

THE DIEPPE RAID

Main image: A German photograph, from a series sold commercially to German personnel, showing Allied prisoners who had been rounded up in the immediate aftermath of the attack on 19 August 1942.

Above: A similar view of Allied prisoners that was taken at the same location, and roughly the same time, as the previous photograph.

Left: A still from a German wartime newsreel showing a survivor of the Dieppe Raid, standing in a landing craft, being offered a drink by a German serviceman in the immediate aftermath of the attack on 19 August 1942.

Opposite page top: Another still from a German newsreel, this image shows Allied prisoners being rounded up in the immediate aftermath of the attack on 19 August 1942. The camouflaged building on the right is the Casino, in this case its eastern end. The turreted building in the centre, the medieval Porte des Tourelles gateway, is on Boulevard de Verdun.

Opposite page bottom: As we have already noted, one of the reporters covering Operation *Jubilee*, from a Royal Navy destroyer, was Drew Middleton. An American employee of the

Associated Press, Middleton is seen here wearing his War Correspondent uniform. Of the withdrawal he would later write the following, which was featured in the Western Daily Press on 21 August 1942: 'We came out escorting lighters full of Canadians. Destroyers laid a smoke screen in front of the town and it was an eerie feeling to move through it and hear the swish of falling bombs. A tank-landing craft, with its motors damaged and steering gear wrecked, asked us for tow. It could make three of our tiny craft, but our skipper took it in his stride. He ran us alongside and directed the crew to fix lines to the tank-landing craft. Once more we were motionless and an easy prey for any German bomber that could sift through the British fighter umbrella. One did get through and two bombs were dropped to our starboard. A fragment from one went through the tiny cabin shared by the ship's two officers. ... With the tank landing craft alongside we started home, looking like a pirate craft, with the crew stripped to the waist in the hot sun and the decks black with blood.'

THE DIEPPE RAID

Left: Two of the landing craft, one containing a Universal Carrier, alongside a destroyer after returning from the beaches during the withdrawal from the beaches at Dieppe.

Above: According to one source, in the front row on the left of this group of prisoners is 'Honorary Captain John Foote, the padre of the Hamilton Light Infantry who was awarded the Victoria Cross for his gallantry in tending to the wounded during the raid.' It is also that Captain David Wesley Clare RCAMC, a medical officer who landed on White Beach, is on the right of the front row. As the historian Charles G. Roland noted, Clare found the enemy 'fire so intense that it was impossible to seek out the wounded. He set up his aid post in the lee of a derelict tank landing craft that had floated in broadside to the beach.' Following his capture, Clare, alongside two other Canadian medical officers and at least one German doctor, soon found himself at work at an improvised medical facility that was established at Verneuil. There, he 'spent two days removing pieces of shrapnel under local anaesthetic, setting fractures, and suturing wounds'.

THE DIEPPE RAID

Right: Allied prisoners beginning their journey into captivity are escorted inland away from the beaches through the streets of Dieppe. Of the Canadian losses, the Canadian Official History contains the following: 'In all categories they totalled 3,367 all ranks. No fewer than 1,946 Canadian officers and men became prisoners of war, at least 568 of them wounded. At Dieppe, from a force of roughly 5,000 men engaged for only nine hours, the Canadian Army lost more prisoners than in the whole eleven months of the later campaign in North-West Europe, or the twenty months during which Canadians fought in Italy. Sadder still was the loss in killed. As now computed, the total of fatal casualties was 56 officers and 851 other ranks; these include seven officers and 65 other ranks who died in captivity, chiefly from wounds received in the operation. Of the seven major Canadian units engaged, only one (Les Fusiliers Mont-Royal) brought its commanding officer back to England – and he ... was badly wounded.'

Below: Another view of British and Canadian prisoners being marched away after *Jubilee*'s end. The effects of the battle they had just endured are clear to see.

Above: With Château de Dieppe towering above them, one group of Allied PoWs, arms raised, is marched away from the beach. In due course, the Germans claimed that a total of 2,217 prisoners were captured at Dieppe. (Polish National Archives)

Below: A group of Allied servicemen are escorted off the beach at Dieppe following the raid on 19 August 1942. In the background is the wrecked Churchill *Burns* - see page 86. (Polish National Archives)

Above: A large number of the Allied personnel captured during the raid were wounded. Of these there is no record except for the Canadians, of whom there were 1,306 unwounded and 568 wounded.

Below: A wounded soldier is carried away by his comrades for treatment, and eventually captivity, on a make-shift stretcher. One man, Stanley Allen Darch, remembers 'walking through broken glass carrying wounded up to the hospital in Dieppe'.

THE DIEPPE RAID

Left: Taken in Rue de Sygogne, the PoWs in this image include Squadron Sergeant-Major Gerald Menzies (No.1 – commander of the tank named *Bert*), Lieutenant Jack Dunlop (No.2 – commander of tank named *Bob*), Lieutenant Bryce Douglas (No.3 – commander of tank *Calgary*), and Trooper Felix Noel (No.4 – crew member of tank *Bert*).

Above: French civilians watch from their doorway as two Canadians head off into captivity. The Canadian War Museum rightly states that the events of 19 August 1942, mark 'Canada's worst single-day loss of the war'.

Overleaf: By mid-afternoon of 19 August, some 500 Canadian PoWs had been corralled together in a park adjacent to the German military hospital located in Avenue Pasteur. There, many of the wounded may well have received some initial medical attention, at least to the extent of applying or changing dressings.

Main image: The individual on the left of the trio of PoWs seen here has been identified as Everett Ross Maracle. Maracle had enlisted in the Essex Scottish Regiment at the age of 16. At the time of the Dieppe Raid, when he held the rank of Lance Corporal, he was believed to be the youngest member of his regiment. When the following account was published in the *Windsor Star* in August 2017, he was said to be the last living Dieppe Raid veteran from his unit:

'"We hit the beach at, I'd say, 4:30 in the morning. It was dark, dusk, yet. Not pitch black, but enough to see the trace of boats coming." Only one of the men Maracle was responsible for was hit – by a bullet to the kneecap. "The others I kept as safe as I could. I cut the barbed wire, I didn't ask them to do it. Got them through that, got them to the firing wall for the rangers, so they could make it up the cliff." But while that was going on, two of Maracle's young friends made a dash through some boulders. "And a German plane swept over them, and machine-gunned them. So they're the two of my best friends who didn't make it." Within 24 hours of landing, the Canadians were forced to surrender. "What could you do?" he asked. "We didn't have no ammunition. Some guys had ammunition, probably two, three rounds left. So that was it." "But, you know, everything is fine now," Maracle said. "I made it. After three years in prison, but we were OK. We came home in one piece."'

THE DIEPPE RAID

THE WITHDRAWAL

Left: A view of the eastern end of the beach at Dieppe after the withdrawal. Soon after the evacuation was completed, General Roberts had sent the following message to the Headquarters 1st Canadian Corps. Despatched by pigeon, it carried the following summary: 'Very heavy casualties in men and ships. Did everything possible to get men off but in order to get any home had to come to sad decision to abandon remainder. This was joint decision by Force Commanders. Obviously operation completely lacked surprise.'

Above: Blindfolded, a German prisoner is guided away into captivity. Another prisoner can be seen behind him over his right shoulder; this second individual would appear to be Unteroffizier Leo Marsiniak who, having been captured at the 'Hess' Battery at Varengeville-sur-Mer, we have encountered previously in Chapter 5.

THE DIEPPE RAID

THE WITHDRAWAL

Left: This group of German prisoners, at least four of whom can be seen in this picture, are landed under guard 'at a South Coast port'.

Below: Two Commandoes share a cigarette on their return to Newhaven.

Above: The Dieppe Victoria Cross holder Major John Weir Foote VC, seen here on the right, is pictured while a guest of honour at a Royal Hamilton Light Infantry dinner on 9 March 1946, barely a month since his award was gazetted. He is chatting with Colonel Denis Whittaker, who commanded the RHLI in Belgium. The latter is showing Major Foote a plaque from a Universal Carrier in which the King rode during a parade held at Aldershot. Foote was the only chaplain to be awarded the Victoria Cross in the Second World War. (Toronto Public Library)

Right: Watched by his wife, Major John Weir Foote VC reads through a handful of the letters of congratulation he reached when the news of his award of the Victoria Cross was announced on 14 February 1946. This photograph was taken two days later.

Chapter 12

THE AFTERMATH

Generalmajor Kurt Zeitzler Chief of Staff Army Group D, France, reported on the immediate aftermath of the raid: 'Although many have already been interred, there are still British dead everywhere, especially in front of our heavy gun positions. In front of one machine-gun post which flanked the narrow strip of beach between the sea and the cliffs, there are piles of dead (more than 100 only in this spot); much booty in equipment and infantry weapons, light and heavy.

'The British fought well … Prisoners make a good impression, young, fresh, intelligent. The aspect of one part of the beach to the west of Dieppe recalls that of Dunkirk. Three large burnt-out transports, high and dry at low tide, with many landing vessels and about 20 tanks which were all knocked out during the landing operations. At other places, still more landing vessels, tanks and funnels and masts sticking out of the water. At Dieppe, damage has been serious at some points, moderate at others. The behaviour of the civil population during the battle has been correct. No cases of sabotage or interference with military measures. Shops re-opened as early as midday on the day of the attack.'[49]

There is no question that the raid was a failure in almost every respect. Of the 6,086 men who landed in France, a total of 3,623, constituting almost 60 per cent, were either killed, wounded, and or taken prisoner. In terms of equipment lost, the Germans listed the following: Twenty-nine Churchill tanks, seven scout cars, one Jeep, a personnel truck, 1,300 rifles, 170 machine-guns (Bren and Sten), forty-two Boys anti-tank rifles, seventy light mortars, sixty heavy mortars, and vast quantities of ammunition, explosives and clothing.

Even the aerial battle with the Luftwaffe was disappointing, with the RAF losing ninety-six aircraft to the Luftwaffe's forty-eight. The Royal Navy lost thirty-three landing craft plus one destroyer, and seventy-five men killed or died of wounds and 269 missing or captured.

There was also an occurrence which was to have long-lasting and brutal consequences. The commanding officer of the Canadian 6th Infantry Brigade, Brigadier William Southam, against explicit orders, took his copy of the assault plan ashore on the main Dieppe beaches. When it became obvious that he would not be able to escape, being unwilling to abandon his men, he sought to bury the assault plan under the pebbles of the beach. But he was spotted by the Germans and when he was taken prisoner, this document was also retrieved. Contained in the plan was an instruction that 'Wherever possible, prisoner's hands will be tied to prevent destruction of their documents', and in apparent confirmation of this were reports of bodies of shot German prisoners found after the battle with their hands tied.

In response to this and following a Combined Operations raid on the Channel Island of Sark, when it was alleged again that German soldiers had been 'shackled', Berlin announced that Allied prisoners, mainly Canadians from Dieppe, would be restrained in a similar fashion.

THE DIEPPE RAID

THE AFTERMATH

Left: By 14.00 hours on 19 August the operation was over. The German artillery had fallen silent two minutes earlier. The meticulous enemy returns indicate that the German gunners had fired 7,458 rounds during the battle, not counting anti-tank and anti-aircraft shells. Here, abandoned armoured vehicles litter the beach at Dieppe after the termination of Operation *Jubilee*. In the centre is a Universal Carrier which the historian Hugh G. Henry states belonged to the Royal Regiment of Canada. Henry adds that it 'was probably under the command of Major McCool', the Principal Military Landing Officer. The Churchill immediately to the right of the Carrier is *Bloody*, while *Blossum* is closest to the camera on the right in the foreground. (National Museum of Denmark)

In warfare, morale, which takes much time to build, can be swept away in moments. The true nature of the losses and failures could not be made known to the Allied public in the immediate aftermath with the outcome of the war still very much in the balance. The raid had to be portrayed as a success, and this communiqué claimed that: 'The raid was a successful demonstration of co-ordination of all three services ... testing by an offensive on a larger scale than previously of the defences of what is known to be a heavily defended sector of the coast, the destruction of German batteries, of a Radiolocation station which plays an important part in the attacks on our Channel convoys, the destruction of German Military Personnel and equipment, and the taking of prisoners for interrogation.'

The Allied press repeated the claims made by Combined Headquarters, announcing that the that Canadian troops had managed to land 'on all the selected spots' and 'took the beach by storm' after sustaining 'a particularly violent resistance on their left flank while they landed tanks at the centre and the right flank quickly reached its objective'.

Above: German personnel inspecting *Cougar* after the Dieppe Raid. A Mk.III, this tank went ashore from TLC 2 (No.127). It was No.13 Troop's leader's tank. Commanded by Lieutenant T.R. Cornett, *Cougar* successfully crossed the beach, having laid its chespaling, and negotiated the seawall up onto the promenade, having only jettisoned part of its Beach Track Laying Device. After turning to the west, it was hit by a 75mm round that jammed its turret.

Below: Another view of *Cougar*, this time clearly showing the Beach Track Laying Device that it was fitted with. After its turret jammed, *Cougar* was only able to engage the tobacco factory with its 6-pounder main armament from its position on the promenade.

Above: Our third view of Lieutenant T.R. Cornett's *Cougar*. Eventually, after having broken one track and having the other blown off by enemy fire, it was destroyed by its crew (they did this by burning out the interior with a sticky bomb supplied for just such a purpose) prior to their retiring back to the beach.

Below: A German soldier examines a Thompson submachine-gun left behind on the beaches at Dieppe. Of the fighting, the Headquarters of the German Fifteenth Army stated the following: 'The large number of English prisoners might leave the impression that the fighting value of the English and Canadian units employed should not be too highly estimated. This is not the case. The enemy, almost entirely Canadian soldiers, fought so far as he was able to fight at all – well and bravely.' (National Museum of Denmark)

THE DIEPPE RAID

Above: Men captured at Dieppe lie in the sun awaiting the next step in their journey into captivity. Though figures vary from source to source, approximately 2,000 men were captured at Dieppe. Of this figure, some 1,874 were Canadian, the rest being British Commandos, Royal Navy officers and seamen, and the like. (Bundesarchiv, Bild 101I-291-1238-10A/Teschendorf/CC-BY-SA 3.0)

Below: This tank, the Mk.III T68176R named *Betty*, was part of 'B' Squadron's 7 Troop. Commanded by Lieutenant A.L. Breithaupt, it fell into a German defensive position by the promenade and could not be rescued.

In fact, all of this had been pre-determined. Whether the raid was a success or a failure, the same conclusions would be drawn. This is to be found in a memorandum presented at a *Jubilee* Communiqué Meeting, which states that 'in the event of much failure, the communiqué [to the press] must then stress the success of the operation as an essential test in the employment of substantial forces and heavy equipment. We then lay extremely heavy stress on stories of personal heroism – through interviews, broadcasts, etcetera – in order to focus public attention on BRAVERY rather than OBJECTIVES NOT ATTAINED.'[50] The capitalisation is in the original document.

The true picture of the raid, however, could not be concealed from the British and Canadian peoples for long. The Germans were quickly able to show, quite literally, the extent of the Allied losses through photographs of the wrecked tanks, the beached and abandoned landing craft and the prisoners being marched into captivity which were reproduced in German newspapers and shared around the world.

To demonstrate this to the British public, two weeks after the raid a four-page A4 size pamphlet with the title *Dieppe – We and British Invade France* was dropped by the Luftwaffe over the UK, chiefly in the south where Canadian troops were based. It contained numerous images of wrecked tanks, Allied PoWs, and dead soldiers and other casualties on the beach.[51]

As Chief of Staff to Hitler's Army Group North, Generalmajor Wilhelm Hasse offered a German perspective on why the raid failed: 'The British completely miscalculated the strength of the German defences and tried to overcome them by landing the main body of their forces, particularly the tanks, right in front of Dieppe. They persisted with this plan though they knew the strength of the defences, concrete constructions, anti-tank walls, machine-gun positions etc. We know this from their [captured] maps.' One element that was not fully appreciated was the German heavy mortars. It was estimated that these mortars accounted for approximately thirty-two per cent of the Allied casualties.[52]

Despite the subsequent claims that were made portraying Dieppe as a vital pre-cursor to the Normandy invasion in 1944, the truth is that the raid was a calamity. Even the official history states that 'it can hardly be claimed that the immediate results were commensurate with the casualties incurred'.[53]

Perhaps surprisingly, though, there were some genuine positives to be drawn from the debacle. The official record found at least one creditable aspect of the raid: 'The Raid showed that we were capable of moving an heterogenous Naval Force of 252 darkened ships and two mine-sweeping flotillas across some 70 miles of sea through an enemy minefield, and of bringing the craft unobserved to their various objectives on time – with two exceptions.' Another is that the raid yielded a copy of *Das Britische Kriegheer* (*The British Army*) which provided the first solid evidence that the Allies' strategic deception campaign to exaggerate its military strength was really working.

But possibly the most telling observation came from the Principal Landing Officer, Major Brian McCool, after his capture. During his two-day interrogation, a German officer asked: 'It was too big for a raid and too small for an invasion. What was it?' To this McCool calmly replied: 'If you can tell me the answer, I would be grateful.'

This view was soon to be repeated in the Allied press as more details about the raid became public knowledge: 'Now the truth is known, we do not believe public opinion in Canada will be satisfied with the official explanation that the raid on Dieppe was instrumental in obtaining crucial information on the defensive organization of the enemy. If the expedition's only goal was to survey coastal defences, one wonders why the same result could not have been achieved with a smaller deployment of troops.'[54]

One of those troops made a similar observation: 'People excused Dieppe by saying, 'Well, we learned by our mistakes'. But we didn't need to make the mistakes we made at Dieppe.'[55]

THE DIEPPE RAID

THE DIEPPE RAID

Previous page: Another view of Lieutenant Breithaupt's *Betty*, this time with the battered buildings of Dieppe's seafront as a backdrop. A post-raid assessment noted that a total of twenty-nine tanks got ashore from the landing craft; of these, two were drowned, and, of the remaining twenty-seven, fifteen crossed the seawall. A report by the German 81st Corps states that eyewitnesses reported that 'probably 16' tanks reached the Promenade. The Commander in-Chief West, however, reported that only five got there; this appears to have been the actual number remaining there after the operation.

Right: A member of Kriegsmarine naval infantry poses with a Canadian machete on the beach at Dieppe after Operation *Jubilee*. He is pictured beside Major Allen Glenn's Mk.I Churchill, *Chief* – as denoted by the F1 in the circle on the turret. Glenn was the OC of 'C' Squadron; his tank was the first ashore.

Below: As soon as the beach and seafront at Dieppe had been declared secure by the defending garrison, then German personnel gradually began arriving to inspect the battlefield. This image shows a particularly large group of officers making their way towards the eastern end of Red beach. The bodies of a few Allied casualties are lying in the foreground; perhaps the lorry on the right is there to undertake their removal? While we cannot be certain, it is possible that the tank that can be seen on the beach in the background is Lieutenant R.H. Wallace's *Backer*.

Above: Further down the beach, this officer is passing LCA 215, which was reported to have been lost during the withdrawal, and the larger hulk of TLC 3. The latter not only transported the tanks of 'B' Squadron's 8 Troop, but also a Caterpillar D7 bulldozer (which was not landed) and the naval and tank beach parties. Soon after the last Churchill, *Beetle*, had disembarked, an enemy shell struck TLC 3's wheelhouse, killing all of the occupants. The ship ended up grounded in shallow water pointing east, about thirty yards west of the tobacco factory. TLC 3 was so badly damaged that she could not be moved.

Opposite: The stern of the beached TLC 3.

Below: Taken by the same photographer as the top image, this shows the scene to the immediate east of the beached TLC 3 and LCA 215. Just beyond the two officers, but in front of the Churchills, is the stranded Daimler Scout car *Helen* of 'B' Squadron's headquarters troop.

THE DIEPPE RAID

Above: German personnel in one of the stranded landing craft at the end of the raid. Note the wounded Allied serviceman lying on the floor at the left side of the opening. The vertical supports on the bows suggest that this might be TLC 3.

Opposite page: An abandoned landing craft on the beach near TLC 3.

Below: Though slightly out of focus, this picture shows German personnel inspecting the debris-littered interior of one of the landing craft.

THE AFTERMATH

Above: German officers and other officials observing the beginning of the recovery and clearance work on Red and White beaches. Note the steel hawsers laid out on the shingle just behind them.

Below: Another of the seventeen LCAs that did not return from the operation. In this case we are looking at the upturned wreck of LCA 294.

Opposite page: This group of visitors, standing on the promenade looking down on to Red and White beaches, were obviously senior enough in rank to warrant the presence of at least two official military photographers. Among the high-ranking officers and officials that visited Dieppe were Sepp Dietrich and Albert Speer, who were duly pictured by one of the knocked-out tanks, that nicknamed *Cat*.

THE DIEPPE RAID

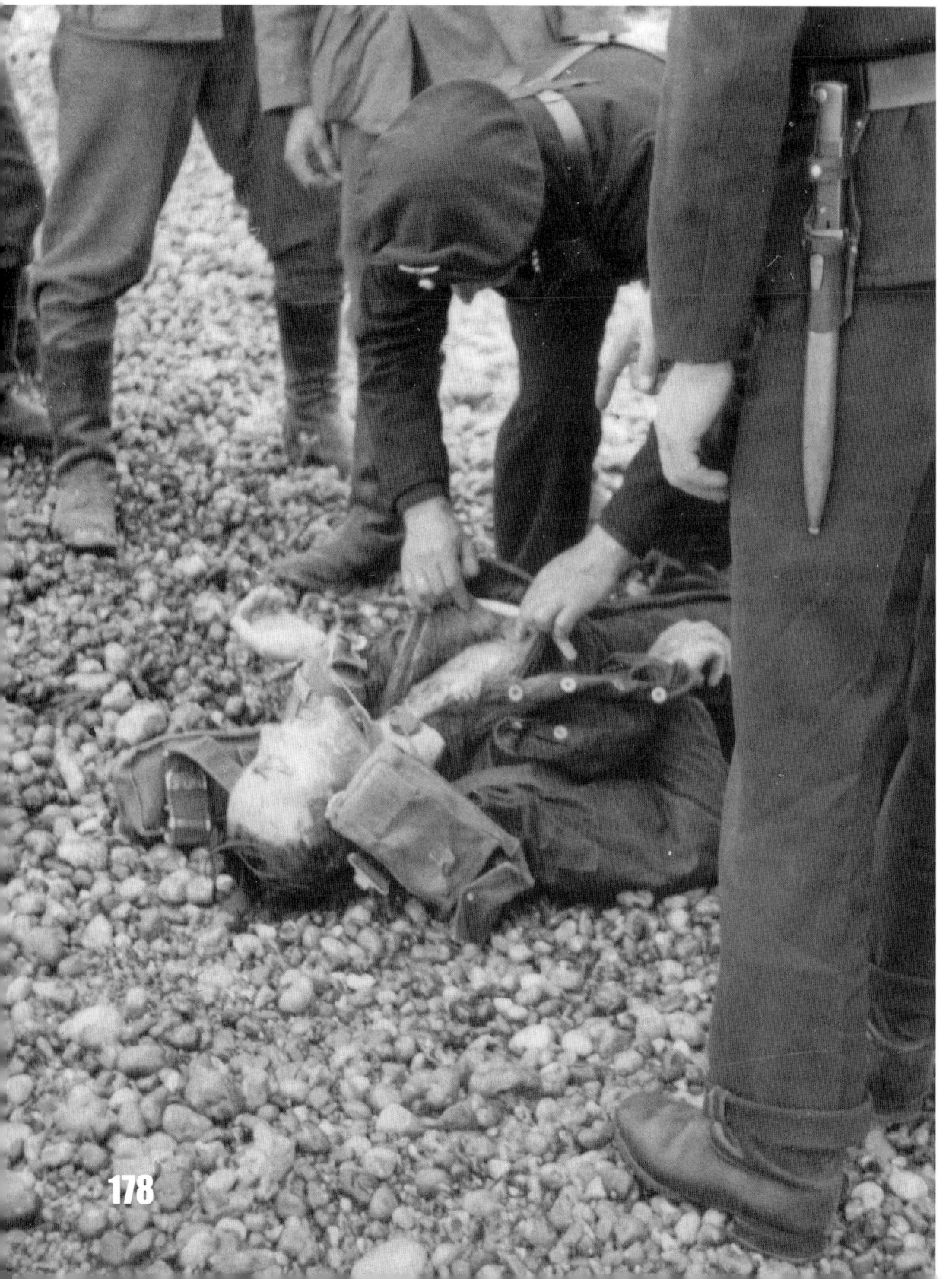

THE AFTERMATH

Above: German personnel walking along the beach near two Churchills. It is possible that it is *Bolster* that can be seen in the centre, the picture perhaps being taken during its recovery.

Opposite page: A group of Germans examine the body of one of the fallen on the beach – it would appear they maybe looking for the casualty's identity discs.

Below: According to one post-war assessment of Operation *Jubilee*, the Germans 'said they had buried about 600 of our [Allied] dead'. It is not known if this funeral service, photographed at Dieppe in the aftermath of the raid, is for Allied or German casualties.

THE DIEPPE RAID

Above: As Oberbefehlshaber West, Generalfeldmarschall Gerd von Rundstedt, seen here on the right with Hitler earlier in 1942, also issued a statement on the Dieppe Raid from his Headquarters. 'The operation at Dieppe cannot be considered a local raid,' he declared. 'For this the expenditure in men and materials is too great. One does not sacrifice twenty to thirty of the most modern tanks for a raid. Much rather is it to be assumed that, by employing such considerable forces, the enemy thought to effect a rapid seizure of the Dieppe bridgehead, after elimination of the artillery defences, in order then to utilise the good port facilities for bringing up and landing in succession the floating and operational reserves.' In summary, von Rundstedt concluded: 'He will not do it like this a second time.' At least on this last point, as events would show two years later, von Rundstedt was entirely correct.
(Polish National Archives)

THE AFTERMATH

Above left: The front cover of the edition of
Picture Post of 5 September 1942, which, covering the Dieppe
Raid, featured one of the returning Commandos on the front. (Robert Mitchell)

Above right: This front page is from an issue of The War Illustrated. The caption to the image states: 'Home from Dieppe after the fierce nine-hour raid by British, US and Fighting French troops on August 19, these two Commandos – battle-stained, but happy – have just stepped ashore at a British port [Newhaven]. They triumphantly display the Union Jack which was planted by one of the first parties of British troops to land in the Dieppe area. The flag acted as a beacon to guide incoming raiders to the landing-stage, and assisted our men to find their way back to the waiting ships.' (Robert Mitchell)

THE DIEPPE RAID

Above: left The front of one of the German 'black' propaganda leaflets that were dropped over Britain in the aftermath of the Dieppe Raid. At the time a radio broadcast instructed people finding such leaflets to hand them in to the Police. This example has the handwritten note 'Leaflet dropped by German plane Aug. 1942.'

Above right: The rear of the German Dieppe Raid propaganda leaflet. The dropping of these by the Luftwaffe was recalled by Ian Coombes who lived in the Witterings near Chichester in West Sussex: 'I remember vividly when the Germans dropped leaflets on us after Dieppe … Of course, we were all gathering up these leaflets, but nobody kept any! They were full of pictures of Canadian soldiers taken prisoner – some of them walking along with no trousers on. It was very upsetting to a great many of us who had become quite friendly with the Canadians during their time here.'

Opposite: Troopers from the Calgary Regiment, pictured after their return to the UK, discuss the events of the raid with a civilian, 23 August 1942.

THE DIEPPE RAID

Above: As the clean-up at Dieppe gets underway, Sergeant T.R. Cunningham's *Bolster* serves as an object of interest to a group of German personnel. By the time this photograph was taken, it would appear that *Bolster* had been moved off the beach.

Opposite page top: Steel hawsers are attached and laid out ready for German engineers to recover the Churchills from the beach. In some cases, this was achieved by using a serviceable Churchill for the towing; there is, for example, at least one picture showing *Bert* being used to pull *Chief* up of the beach onto the promenade. We can see that the tank second from the right, facing the photographer, is *Bill*. This could mean that the next Churchill to the left is *Bob*, with to the left of that *Calgary*.

Opposite page bottom: Waves lap at the tracks of Lieutenant Douglas' *Calgary*. Douglas had recently been appointed as 'C' Squadron's reconnaissance officer. The last tank off its landing craft, *Calgary* towed the Daimler Scout car *Horace* ashore. Visible directly behind and above *Calgary*, fully submerged to the top of its hull, is *Bill*. The third Churchill in this view, on the right, is *Bob*.

THE AFTERMATH

THE DIEPPE RAID

THE AFTERMATH

Left: The view on the seafront at Dieppe following the raid on 19 August 1942. The image is taken looking east along what is today the Boulevard de Verdun. Note the distinctive, and camouflaged, towers of the Porte des Tourelles on the right foreground. The Casino is to the left of this view. In his book *Dieppe 1942: The Jubilee Disaster* the author Ronald Atkin states that such was the scale of the damage caused in the town by the raid that Hitler presented the sum of ten million Francs to go towards the cost of the repairs.

Above: Among the many who were decorated or honoured for their part in the Dieppe Raid were Corporal Alfred Daoust (on the left), of Les Fusiliers Mont-Royal, and Sergeant E.L. Dixon, of The Essex Scottish Regiment, both of whom received the Military Medal during an investiture at Buckingham Palace on 27 October 1942.

THE DIEPPE RAID

Left: Having attended the same ceremony as Daoust and Dixon, Major Marie-Edmond Paul Garneau, of the Royal 22e Regiment, was awarded the Distinguished Service Order for 'gallant and distinguished services in the combined attack on Dieppe'.

Below: Also pictured outside Buckingham Palace after the investiture ceremony on 27 October 1942, is Brigadier Sherwood Lett, MC, ED, who received the Distinguished Service Order, again for 'gallant and distinguished service at Dieppe'. To the left is Mrs. Charles Banks; to the right, Nursing Sister Hilda Boutilier of Sydney, Nova Scotia.

THE DIEPPE RAID

Above: A pair of German handcuffs worn by Allied PoWs in Stalag Luft VIII-B at Lamsdorf in the aftermath of the Dieppe Raid. Following the German instructions that Allied prisoners should be handcuffed, in the camp this was originally done by tying the hands together using cord from Red Cross parcels. In time, manacles such as these, which are believed to have been worn by Corporal George Desforges, became available to the camp authorities. The shackling lasted thirteen months. Some of the prisoners, displaying their usual ingenuity, found ways of removing the manacles. For example, they fashioned keys from the 'can-openers' attached to tins of sardines supplied in the Red Cross food parcels. This pair can be seen on display in the Lashenden Air Warfare Museum. (Courtesy of Robert Mitchell)

Opposite page: Two Dieppe prisoners can be seen in this picture taken at a Red Cross party held on 28 March 1945, following their liberation. Howard 'Red' Gorle is on the left, Bill Stevens on the right. Between them is Flight Lieutenant Don Morrison, DFC, DFM, who was shot down and crashed in Germany. Serving in the Royal Regiment of Canada, Gorle had landed on Blue beach. While ashore he was hit and badly wounded in his right shoulder. Moments before he was hit, a man standing next to him, 20-year-old Private Charles 'Kenny' Wright was shot and died in Gorle's arms. (Toronto Public Library)

THE AFTERMATH

THE DIEPPE RAID

Above: Canadian troops returned to Dieppe on 1 September 1944, this being the date that the town was, fittingly, liberated by the men of the 2nd Canadian Division. This image shows Major J.M. Figott and members of the Royal Hamilton Light Infantry kneeling at the graves of Canadian soldiers killed in the raid two years earlier. (Canada Department of National Defence/Library and Archives Canada/PA-176696)

REFERENCES AND NOTES

1. L.M. Maisky, *Memoirs of a Soviet Ambassador: The War, 1939-43* (Hutchinson, London, 1967), p.270.
2. Arthur Bryant, *The Turn of the Tide, 1939-1943* (Collins, London, 1957), p.340.
3. ibid, pp.359-60.
4. Brian Loring Villa, *Unauthorized Action, Mountbatten and the Dieppe Raid* (Oxford University Press, 1994), p.166.
5. Field Marshal Sir B.L. Montgomery, *Memoirs of Field-Marshal Montgomery* (Collins, London, 1958), p.76.
6. Despite claims that the remounting of the raid was not authorised, this is demonstrably untrue. *The Dieppe Raid: The Combined Operations Assault on Hitler's European Fortress, August 1942* (Frontline, Barnsley, 2019), p.10.
7. Terence Robertson, *The Shame and the Glory* (Little Brown, London, 1963), p.75.
8. Published by Harper & Row in 1975.
9. The National Archives (TNA), CAB 120/65, Meeting with M. Stalin, arrangements, meetings and papers; TNA PREM 3/76N12 Records of Cairo and Moscow conferences.
10. Nigel West. 'Jubilee or Betrayal', in *Unreliable Witness: Espionage Myths of the Second World War* (Weidenfeld & Nicolson, London, 1984), p.130.
11. *The Dieppe Raid*, op. cit., Appendix G.
12. Colonel C.P. Stacey, *The Canadian Army 1939-1945, An Official Historical Summary*, (Department of National Defense), p.70.
13. Brereton Greenhous, 'Operation Flodden: The Sea Fight off Berneval and the Suppression of the Goebbels Battery, 19 August 1942', *Canadian Military Journal* (Autumn, 2003), p.50.
14. Robin Neillands, *The Dieppe Raid: The Story of the Disastrous 1942 Expedition* (Aurum Press, London, 2006), p.140.
15. ibid.
16. Quoted from Lord Lovat, *March Past* (Frontline Book, Barnsley, 2022).
17. Hugh G. Henry, *The Planning, Intelligence, Execution and Aftermath of the Dieppe Raid, 19 August 1942* (St John's College University of Cambridge, 1996), p.251.
18. TNA, DEFE 2/337.
19. *The London Gazette* (Supplement), No.35729, 2 October 1942, p.4323.
20. TNA, DEFE 2/337.
21. 'Commando Raid on Varengeville, France' in *Tactical and Technical Trends* No.28, 1 July 1943.
22. *The Dieppe Raid*, op. cit., p.27.
23. Henry, op cit, p.238.
24. Terence Robertson, p.294.
25. ibid, p.116.
26. Colonel C.P. Stacey, *Six Years of War: The Army in Canada, Britain and the Pacific* (Department of National Defence, Ottawa), pp.363-4.

27 See veterans.gc.ca/eng/video-gallery/video/9681.
28 *The Dieppe Raid*, op. cit., p.29.
29 William Whitehead, *Dieppe 1942, Echoes of Disaster* (Richard Drew, Glasgow, 1982), p.105.
30 Jack Nissen, *Winning the Radar War* (Robert Hale, London, 1987), p.152.
31 Naval Staff History, Battle Summary No.33, 'Raid on Dieppe'.
32 ibid, p.31.
33 ibid.
34 Hugh G. Henry, 'The Calgary Tanks at Dieppe', *Canadian Military History*, Volume 4, Issue 1, 1995.
35 TNA WO 179/1156.
36 The full story of the actions of the tanks at Dieppe can be seen in Hugh G. Henry's *Dieppe Through the Lens of the German War Photographer* (After the Battle, London).
37 TNA, WO 179/1156.
38 Johannes Jörgensen (Translated by Andreas Gropp and Krista Grop), 'Dieppe From the Other Side: German Newspaper Accounts of the Raid', *Canadian Military History*, Volume 21, Issue 4, 2015.
39 Nissen, op cit, pp.187-8.
40 *The Dieppe Raid*, op. cit.
41 'The Dieppe Raid at 80: An Airman's Account', www.cwgc.org/our-work/blog/the-dieppe-raid-at-80-an-airman-s-account/
42 A.B. Austin, *We Landed At Dawn* (Angus and Robertson, Sydney, 1943), p.103.
43 Quoted from 'The RAF at Dieppe', www.keymilitary.com/article/raf-dieppe.
44 Account provided by Leopold Wenger to the author and historian Chris Goss.
45 *The Dieppe Raid*, op. cit.
46 Norman Franks, *The Greatest Air Battle: Dieppe, 19th August 1942* (William Kimber, London, 1979), p.14.
47 Nissen, op cit.
48 *The London Gazette* (Supplement), 12 February 1946, p.941.
49 Naval Staff History, Battle Summary No.33.
50 Quoted in Timothy Balzer, 'In Case the Raid Is Unsuccessful ... Selling Dieppe to Canadians', *The Canadian Historical Review* 87, 3, September 2006, University of Toronto Press.
51 Austin J. Ruddy, *Britain at War* Magazine, 25 July 2019.
52 Thompson, p.191.
53 *The Dieppe Raid*, p.51.
54 'Les leçons de Dieppe,' *La Patrie*, 16 September 1942, p.10, in Béatrice Richard, 'Dieppe The Making of a Myth', *Canadian Military History*, Volume 21, Issue 4, 2015.
55 Whitehead, op cit, p.157.